Putting on the Mind of Christ

Putting on the Mind of Christ

Contemplative Prayer and Holistic Unity

James E. Woods

ORBIS BOOKS
Maryknoll, New York 10545

ORBIS BOOKS
Maryknoll, New York 10545

Fathers and Brothers
MARYKNOLL™

Founded in 1970, Orbis Books endeavors to publish works that enlighten the mind, nourish the spirit, and challenge the conscience. The publishing arm of the Maryknoll Fathers and Brothers, Orbis seeks to explore the global dimensions of the Christian faith and mission, to invite dialogue with diverse cultures and religious traditions, and to serve the cause of reconciliation and peace. The books published reflect the views of their authors and do not represent the official position of the Maryknoll Society. To learn more about Orbis Books, please visit our website at www.orbisbooks.com.

Library of Congress Cataloging-in-Publication Data

Names: Woods, James E. (Pastor), author.
Title: Putting on the mind of Christ : contemplative prayer and holistic
  unity / James E. Woods.
Description: Maryknoll, New York : Orbis Books, 2021. | Includes
  bibliographical references and index. | Summary: "Putting on the Mind of
  Christ examines the biblical, historical, scientific, and theological
  aspects of contemplative prayer and mysticism that have the effect of
  changing our outlook on the world and seeing God and neighbor as a
  holistic unity"— Provided by publisher.
Identifiers: LCCN 2020031302 (print) | LCCN 2020031303 (ebook) | ISBN
  9781626984233 (trade paperback) | ISBN 9781608338863 (epub)
Subjects: LCSH: Contemplation. | Mysticism. | Prayer—Christianity.
Classification: LCC BV5091.C7 W66 2021 (print) | LCC BV5091.C7 (ebook) |
  DDC 248.3/4—dc23
LC record available at https://lccn.loc.gov/2020031302
LC ebook record available at https://lccn.loc.gov/2020031303

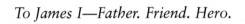
To James I—Father. Friend. Hero.

Contents

Foreword

On Being a Contemplative Christian

You are my Beloved, in whom I am well pleased!

These are the words that Jesus heard as he was coming up out of the waters of the River Jordan after having been baptized by his cousin John (cf. Mark 1:9–11). The good news that Jesus came to deliver to the world, which he proclaimed in his words and actions and to which he himself witnessed with his own life, and more specifically with his passion, death, and resurrection, is precisely this very message of *unconditional Love*, given to us all, the entirety of God's creation—yes, every single one of us, each in our own unique way. *You are my Beloved, in whom I am well pleased!*

It is not something we have to earn, something that we need to work for in order to obtain. On the contrary, it is a free and bounteous gift of grace given to each and every one of us created by the loving will of God and in God's own image. We only have to accept it, welcome it fully into our lives, and live in its light. This acceptance is what we call faith, and it is what makes us Christian. Not through any special virtue or achievement on our part, but by a sheer gift of grace. To repeat: this unconditional Love is not a prize for our efforts or any achievement we can claim for ourselves, but a totally gratuitous gift. All we can do is accept this gift in all humility, rejoice, and give thanks for the rest of our lives as we endeavor to live in accordance with that Love. We do so in the way we go about our ordinary human lives, in the ways we relate to one another, to the whole of creation, and to our own selves. This is behind what Paul the Apostle tells the Thessalonians, "Rejoice, pray without ceasing, give thanks always, for this is the will of God for you in Jesus Christ" (1 Thess 5:16–18).

Our ultimate destiny as human beings is simply to delight and bask in that unconditional Divine Love for all eternity, together with all those beloved of God who have freely accepted that Love and have somehow lived it in their lives. This ultimate destiny is also described as the Beatific Vision, that is, directly beholding the face of God in communion with all the saints in a state of bliss and joy in infinite capacity, thoroughly immersed in that Love. This is the culmination and final fulfillment of an inherent desire rooted within each of us, a deep-seated yearning embedded in our hearts attested to by philosophers and theologians, psychologists and psychotherapists, and others, a yearning that mistakenly drives us to all kinds of earthly pursuits, of pleasure, of possessions, of power, or what have you, toward its satisfaction, but to no avail. Our earthly human hearts, as Saint Augustine aptly wrote in his *Confessions,* are "restless, until they rest in Thee," that is, in the infinite Triune Mystery we call God, the source and fount of all Truth, Goodness, Beauty, and Love. That is reason to rejoice indeed, and give thanks.

"Praying without ceasing," contemplative prayer, enables us to access, experience, and activate the dynamic reality of this Divine Love, in which we are all immersed right from the start. It is an intentional and cultivated attitude that we can take on from our side, to enable the eyes of our heart to see "the things of God" clearly and without obstruction in all things around us.

The word "contemplation" is a Latin-based term derived from the Greek verb *theorein,* which means "to see, to behold."

We find this usage many times in the Fourth Gospel, such as in the passages: "one who, seeing (*theōrōn*) me, sees (*theōrei*) the One who sent me" (John 12:45), and "all who, seeing (*theōrōn*) the Son and believe, shall have eternal life" (John 6:40). Scripture scholars note nuances in the meaning of this verb, which include "gazing thoroughly," "looking at in a concentrated way," and "a lingering, considering, deliberate way of beholding (and believing)." Contemplative prayer is thus a way for us to soak ourselves in the ever-present reality of Divine Love being poured out to each and every one of us unconditionally and in profusion.

The psalmist offers a very concise and direct pointer to contemplative prayer: "Be still, and know that I am God" (Ps 46:10). In other words, let your inquisitive, analyzing, comparing, judging, grasping mind desist from all its fruitless activity, and let it quiet down, let it return to a simple awareness of things as they are, in tranquility, in clarity. And in that stillness, you will know: "I AM" (Exod 3:14). To bask in the Divine Presence, to be immersed in unconditional Love, is the heart of contemplative prayer. "Taste and see how good is the LORD!" (Ps 34:8).

This is a glimpse, a foretaste of the Beatific Vision, our ultimate destiny, wherein the veil will finally be lifted from our eyes and we shall behold the face of God in joy and bliss in infinite measure.

This foretaste of that Divine Love without measure that awaits us in eternity and may be given to us every now and then in contemplative prayer is not meant to make us just sit smugly and wait passively for its fruition in the hereafter. On the contrary, it enables us to behold this earthly realm wherein we continue to live our human lives no longer from our egoic, self-centered minds, but with the eyes of the heart and mind of Jesus, a heart burning with Divine Love that touches and transforms us, inviting us to embrace this wounded world and fill it with that Love. Not our own little human love, but the Divine

Love that works in and through us, transforming us and allowing us in our own puny and limited way to participate in the divine movement of embracing the world and bringing it home to Itself.

Those graced with having heard the good news of God's unconditional Love, seeking to live fully in its light, are also entrusted with this singular mission, echoed in a popular song: "to fill the world with Love one's whole life through." This is what spreading and witnessing to this good news "to the ends of the earth" (Acts 1:8), "to all creation" (Mark 16:15) entails.

In sum, to be a contemplative Christian is to open the eyes of one's heart to the Love that fills the world, to be enlightened and empowered by it in every thought, word, and action one takes. It is "putting on the mind of Christ" to become an instrument of that Love, participating in the manifold tasks involved in healing and transforming our broken world.

We are all indebted to James E. Woods for gifting us with this volume, providing for us the scriptural, historical, theological, and practical underpinnings of what it takes to be a contemplative Christian, to put on the mind of Christ.

Ruben L. F. Habito
March 15, 2020

Acknowledgments

It is basically an impossible task to thank all those who have helped make this project a reality. Nevertheless, at the risk of omitting names that should undoubtedly appear here, I'm compelled to try.

Above all, I give thanks to the Divine Mystery, the true source of all creativity, in whom we "live and move and have our being." In a contemplative posture of awe, there are literally no words to express the gratitude and humility I have for God granting me the privilege to produce this work.

Second, I pay homage to my wife, Mia, who continues to see things in me long before I see them myself. It is not an exaggeration to say that, without her, none of this could have happened. She's read papers in which she has had little to no interest; she's listened to complaints, many of which were unfounded; and she's spent days on end with minimal attention. All the while she smiled, catered, and encouraged. She remains my literal and figurative "life editor."

In the same vein I salute my children—James III, Daniel, and Phoebe. Not only are they constant inspirations, but they have tolerated my distance and moodiness throughout this entire project. I am proud of the beautiful human beings they are, and the lives they have yet to lead.

Sticking to the theme of family, I thank my mother, LeeEtta, who, like many women in human history, kept the faith alive and ensured our family and faith traditions cascaded from generation to generation; she taught me to love unconditionally. For my sister, Andréa, I simply say, "*Namaste*."

Next is my editor, Paul McMahon. His patience and kindness were manifest as he shepherded me through the publishing process from start to finish. He is an extraordinary wordsmith and interpreter of esoteric ideas (sometimes scarily so!). I am indebted to his genius.

Given the theological nature of this work, I must credit the faculty past and present at SMU's Perkins School of Theology who laid the foundation and set the plumb line for this venture. As an advisor, mentor, and mystic, Ruben Habito opened doors that I didn't know existed, then he gently extended a hand of invitation for me to pass through their portals. Carlos Cardoza-Orlandi prodded me to understand the depths of scholarship, remaining a constant voice of reassurance. James Lee's reverence for the mystics and his impressive teaching style left an indelible mark on my outlook. Roy Heller taught me to how to ask my own questions and examine the answers to them. Robert Foster, Abraham Smith, and Sze-kar Wan unlocked the mysteries of scripture through language and context. Ted Campbell helped me to appreciate the current and future relevance of things past. Elaine Heath provided a framework for me to understand the faith as an invitation to mission. Alyce McKenzie illuminated the sacred calling and task of ministry, especially as it relates to storytelling. Rebekah Miles (and her father, John) gave me insight into why theology matters. And Jessica Boon reinforced the essential notion that an argument is a fool's errand if it doesn't answer the fundamental question of "So what?"

Also related to academia, I need to pass along a heartfelt thanks to Magdalena Grohman at the University of Texas at Dallas; she selflessly provided much-needed guidance for the neuro-psychological portions of this work.

The community of faith at First United Methodist Church of McKinney, Texas, is also due my gratitude. As senior pastor, Tommy Brumett allows for freedom in ministry and creativity in its application; he continues to serve as a mentor and a friend. As a field supervisor and reader for my doctoral studies, John Harman ensured that I kept the delicate balance of scholarship and parish ministry. Don Renshaw helped launch my pastoral career and steadied my early efforts with a unique mix of strength and gentleness. Meanwhile, the remaining clergy members, Janet, Patty, Stacey, "Good" Chris, "Bad" Kris, Ed, and Abe continue to support me in numerous ways, and I value their counsel. I also give thanks to the Living Faith adult class, members past and present of the Disciple™ formation classes, the Wednesday evening Communion Chapel congregants, and the steering committee members of the Center for Transformative Prayer. All have directly or indirectly informed this work.

I also owe a deep debt to the Cistercian-Trappist community at Assumption Abbey in Ava, Missouri. Brother Francis took me under his wing as my spiritual director the moment I first ventured into that Ozark enclave. Father Thaddeus welcomed me into the community, and all the priests and brothers there continue to serve as a source of living contemplative nourishment. I am also thankful for Family Brothers John Douglas and John Ockels for paving the way, and for Father Paul whose life transition from Methodist minister to Catholic priest formed an ecumenical bridge across which many have connected.

All of our lives are formed at an early age, but especially when we leave home and have to make our way in the world ourselves. For that reason I recognize the love and support of David Poulos, Dennis Stotts, Paul Martinez, Ben Quindoza, Dan Baca, David Sanchez, David San Juan, Jim Archuleta, Steve Muth, Heather Ainsworth, Shelley Walker, Randy Black, John Sinovic, and Ashraf Bseisu for thirty-five years of connection that has transcended the words "friendship" or "fictive kin," and evolved to true family. I also thank Darrin Wesley, a brother for over forty years; Max Gilreath, John Ayo, and Irfan Ahmed as gifted listeners; Lynn Fabia and Michael Park, teachers and mentors; and the leaders of the Rising Spirit Aikido family, Bob and Caren Coffel, Kevin Scott, and Bill Stynetski, for tolerating my thinly veiled "preaching" for nearly twenty years.

Finally, I express deep gratitude for the family, friends, teachers, and bountiful cloud of witnesses whose names do not explicitly appear here, but upon whose unending love I have always relied.

Introduction

A clergy member of a mainline Protestant church approached several parishioners to voluntarily participate in a nonscientific "experiment" on prayer. During an orientation gathering, the pastor provided an intentionally vague description of the study and its contents, because he wanted to minimize the bias that could occur from his interaction with the volunteers. However, he did allude to the fact that these daily prayers would be "contemplative" in nature. Noticing one member's furrowed brow on hearing this label, he asked if she had any questions or concerns. Her response, while a typical one, was yet immensely instructive: "I understand prayer as a conversation with God; but that means I usually ask God for my needs, and then I wait for a response. What is 'contemplative' prayer?"

Prayer is a mainstay of Christian life and practice. While not unique to Christianity, it is foundational to our relationship with God. We commonly pray over meals and bow our heads before we lie down to sleep. We lift liturgical prayers in worship and utter brief, gentle thanks under our breath. Prayer is a primary vehicle of growth in the faith journey. But while we are seemingly intimate with the concept of prayer, we often frame it in a monolithic mold, lacking any substance or nuance.

The English word "prayer" comes from the Latin word *precari*, meaning "to beg," "to implore," or "to entreat."[1] As narrow as that definition seems, there are several major categories of prayer within scripture. *Petitions* and *supplications* are requests made for ourselves or on behalf of someone else (cf. Job 6:8; Phil 4:6); *confessions* are cries to God in an appeal for mercy (cf. Ps 51; Luke 18:13); and the related prayers of *praise* and *thanksgiving* glorify God for God's sake (cf. 1 Sam 2:1–10; Luke 1:46–55), or express gratitude for the blessings we enjoy (cf. Ps 75; 1 Thess 1:2). Each of these has a unique function in the Christian's communication with the Divine, and most of those who pray are familiar with these categories. However, distinct from such classifications, our *approach* to the devotional life differentiates the depth and character of how prayer informs and shapes our daily lives.

The apostle Paul implores the church at Thessalonica to "pray without ceasing" (1 Thess 5:17; cf. Luke 18:1). Given that this plea cannot be taken literally according to the categories of prayer described above, Paul must have a different understanding of prayer. A clue to his intent is woven within his explanation of why his audience should pray constantly: "for this is the will of God in Christ Jesus for you" (1 Thess 5:18). Consequently, attending to the divine will is ostensibly the purpose of unremitting communication with God. The *classification* of prayer is not the central focus; rather it forms the proper *orientation* or *attitude* of those who pray. The intent of prayer is not a temporary mindset adopted solely for occasional pauses to clasp our hands or bow our heads, nor is it a method or a style to be employed when the mood hits. Rather, it is about an approach; it is a permanent mentality of offering all our daily goings on as a continuous attentiveness to God—it is *life* as prayer. Contemplative prayer is grounded in this awareness.

Contemplative prayer is not so much concerned with types or even methods or techniques as it is with the disposition of the heart. Certainly, while there are different methodical ways the contemplative goes about cultivating this heart through prayer, the aim of contemplation is "an unconditional and totally humble surrender to God, a total acceptance of ourselves and of our situation" as willed by the Divine.[2] If prayer is communication—a "conversation," as popularly framed—then the contemplative frequently adopts the role of *listener*, eager to be silent and to hear what God has to say. Interestingly, data suggests this receptive mode to be lacking in the United States.

A June 2017 survey of just over one thousand adults (nearly 90 percent of whom professed to be Christian) reflects that the respondents' prayers were contemplative for only 8 percent of the time. By contrast, an overwhelming majority of prayer in the United States was characterized as a "solitary activity defined primarily by the immediate needs and concerns of the individual."[3] These statistics argue for a severely myopic view, one that has the potential to nurture a negative sense of ambition and self-centeredness—concepts alien to Christian virtue. Furthermore, this approach to prayer risks making the conversation about ourselves, a monologue that disconnects us from the source on whom we unescapably rely.

In his now classic work titled *Prayer*, the late contemplative Abhishiktananda aptly observes that prayer "is to see God, to recognize and adore his presence and his glory in everything."[4] Such a definition of prayer is consistent with Paul's counsel to pray always, living life as prayer. It requires, however, a renewed approach to prayer—one that is not opposed to personal petitions or other types, but incorporates their purpose and intent into a larger way of being and seeing. Abhishiktananda lends further depth:

> To pray without ceasing is much less to think about God all the time than to act continually under the direction of his Spirit. It is to live and act "in Christ" (Gal 2:20); or better still, *it is to allow Jesus freely to live in us his life as Son of God....* It is to answer with Jesus, "Yes, Father," full of faith and love, *in every conscious act of our life* (emphasis added).[5]

Such prayer requires a worldview in which we see ourselves united with Christ, each other, and all creation. This union has already been made real through the work of the cross, but many have yet to assume this "mind of Christ." Ironically, prayer itself assists us in attaining this adoption, and there is something inherent specifically to the practice of contemplation that influences this unitive experience of ourselves, God, and the world. As such, contemplative prayer plays a foundational role in the formation of a unitive perception of reality.

In the following chapters, we examine this assertion from multiple perspectives, using disparate academic disciplines as a basis for critical analysis. The first chapter sets out the discussion, restating the argument and providing critical *definitions* to provide clarity at the point of embarkation. Chapter 2 begins the excursion in earnest, locating the *biblical* foundations of the thesis. It grounds the virtuous aim of Christian unitive perception and presents contemplative prayer as a tool in achieving that end, consistent with the biblical record in practice and function. Chapter 3 demonstrates the embodiment of these tenets in the life of a *historical* figure taken from the "mystical" tradition of Eastern Christianity and buttresses the argument of contemplation's transformative qualities, highlighting the background, salient works, contemplative practices, and resulting unitive perception of the mystic. Chapter 4 explores this practice's mental impacts from a *neuropsychological* perspective, identifying the physiological processes that help determine "self" and describing the shift in our sense of reality resulting from changes to those neural structures. Chapter 5 provides a *theological* synthesis of our work, following the path of prayer as it echoes the passion, death, and resurrection of Christ. It also presents a concept of atonement as a natural outgrowth of those observations. We conclude with a final commentary on the "next steps" of Christian education on contemplation.

1

First Things

As the mainline pastor sought out participants for his study, one parishioner was particularly eager to join, and she readily signed up. She had been exposed to meditation and other centering practices during years of yoga instruction, so she thought this might be something that would resonate with that experience. Yet, while being completely open to the idea of contemplative prayer, she maintained a slight sense of uncertainty—she was unfamiliar with this new terminology and practice as it related to her Christian context. She needed a frame of reference.

BEFORE EXPLORING THE TOPIC IN DEPTH, we must first understand three key concepts. First, we will explore the concept of the "*mind of Christ.*" There are diverse ways this phrase can be interpreted; our focus will be on two Pauline texts and the Gospels. Second, we will explore the meaning of *unitive perception*—a somewhat ethereal term—within a Christian context using author and Episcopal priest Cynthia Bourgeault's notion of "nondual consciousness." Finally, we will explore the idea of *contemplative prayer* itself, identifying some of its unique characteristics within the larger backdrop of prayer. We will also briefly consider some arguments against this practice and subsequently address those concerns.

The "Mind of Christ"

In the Letter to the Philippians, Paul cites what some biblical scholars believe to be a standing Christian "hymn," an oral tradition that is presumably known by others within the faith (Phil 2:6–11).[1] While the content of this passage has implications for our overall topic, Paul's preface to the hymn sets the tone. The author writes, "Let the same mind be in you that was in Christ Jesus" (Phil 2:5). This provocative statement begs the question: What is the "mind of Christ"?

The NRSV translation of the Pauline letters renders two different Greek terms as "mind." In Philippians, the underlying word, *phroneo*, occurs eight times (vv. 1:7; 2:2 twice, 5; 3:15, 19; 4:2, 10), indicating its overall significance. While the term has slightly different meanings depending on context, in this letter *phroneo* is limited to two meanings, the predominant one being an "attitude" or "disposition" (2:2, 5; 3:15, 19; 4:2).[2] The attitude to which Paul alludes is described by Christ's actions at the core of the hymn.

Verses 6 to 8 of the Philippians passage speak directly to a disposition of *humility* and *selflessness*. Paul seemingly detects an atmosphere of self-centeredness in the community, and so he issues a corrective note for those who claim to be "in Christ."[3] He reminds the church that Christ selflessly "emptied" (v. 7) himself of his Godly estate and "humbled" himself through "obedience" (v. 8). This act of humility is *intentional*, a voluntary movement that recognizes agency in the one who submits.[4] The attitude that God glorifies in the end is one of "self-denying service for others to the point of death with no claim of return, no eye upon reward."[5] For Paul, to have the "mind of Christ" means a full participation in Christ, but specifically in his actions related to the cross. Paul's letter to the Corinthians confirms this interpretation.

2

In 1 Corinthians 2, Paul argues that those in the faith have the power to discern the mysteries of God, not because of an innate ability to plumb the divine depths, but because "we have the mind of Christ" (1 Cor 2:16). While this claim may seem audacious, vetting the text reveals Paul's rationale. In this passage, the word used for "mind" is *noun*, a term similar to our common understanding of a "faculty of thinking," an intellectual capacity, or the sum of the "mental and moral state of being."[6] However, searching further reveals an additional meaning that resonates with our purposes. Some scholars note that when Paul uses the term "mind" here, he is using it interchangeably with the word "spirit."[7] Because this "mind" is Spirit-filled *in* Christ, it is thereby virtually indistinguishable from that *of* Christ. It possesses God's wisdom of revelation, a wisdom, which, for Paul, equates solely to Christ crucified (1 Cor 1:23–24; 2:2).[8] To have the "mind of Christ," then, is inseparable from participating in the cross. But to what end?

Ultimately, the humility and selflessness that are characteristic of the "Christ mind" promote a loving *unity* within the community. Clues to this goal emerge in Philippians 2:3, with Paul admonishing the church at Philippi to check their motivations of "selfish ambition" and "conceit." They are to look instead toward the "interests of others" (2:4). He later exhorts them to "be of the same mind," focused on the prize of Christ (3:14–15). This idea of communal unity is even more evident in Paul's message to the Corinthians. Early in the letter, he petitions the church to put away divisions and be "united in the same mind and the same purpose" (1 Cor 1:10). His appeal is laid bare in chapter 3 where he calls to task those who are divided over petty allegiances (vv. 4–9, 21–23). Divisiveness is anathema to the community of believers. Unity, therefore, represents the distinguishing mark of those who share in the "mind of Christ." And while Paul's theology does not call for imitation of the "historical" person of Jesus, the gospel writers neverthe-less confirm that this overall attitude of humility and selflessness is espoused and embodied by Christ.[9]

In the Gospel of Matthew, Jesus counsels the crowd to "strive first for the kingdom of God and his righteousness, and all these things will be given to you as well" (Matt 6:33). This striving requires humility and obedience, so Christ sets the ex-ample by washing his disciples' feet (cf. John 13:3–16). Such acts of humility lend themselves to selflessness, and in Mark, Jesus expresses his greatest act of selflessness, saying: "For the Son of Man came not to be served but to serve, and to give his life as a ransom for many" (Mark 10:45). Finally, as Paul's the-ology suggests, an attitude of humility and selflessness encour-ages a condition of unity. According to John, in Jesus's final prayer before his passion, he states:

> The glory that you have given me I have given them, *so that they may be one, as we are one, I in them and you in me, that they may become completely one*, so that the world may know that you have sent me and have loved them even as you have loved me. (John 17:22–23; emphasis added)

Unity is significant, for, through its realization, we are par-ticipating in Christ, and this participation makes us "completely one" in the love of God.

With these brief sketches from Paul and the Gospels as our guide, we can render our working definition of the "mind of Christ." The "mind" conforms to the disposition and the "spirit" of Jesus, the archetype of humanity. It is characterized by *humility*, a portal through which *selflessness* readily flows. Being "other-oriented," as such, the boundaries of "self" ex-pand ever outward, becoming virtually limitless. And from this location of inclusivity, this "mind" perceives a loving sense of *unity*, a state of divine intimacy whose bounds are undefined.

UNITIVE PERCEPTION

As we have noted, the "mind of Christ" presupposes a unified view of the world. In John's Gospel, for example, we find Jesus praying on behalf of the faithful, "that they may be one" (John 17:21). This is a prayer for solidarity, a harmonious condition that is both rooted in and compelled by love. But the "oneness" for which Jesus appeals is no ordinary camaraderie; it is nothing short of our full participation in the Divine. He continues his plea, "As you, Father, are in me and I am in you, may they also be in us..." (John 17:21). Comprehending this cosmic unity is no mere act of the intelligence. The "mind of Christ" presupposes a different way of knowing.

Ewert Cousins describes the human spirit as the "deepest center" of our being, that part of us that is "open to the transcendent" and "experiences the ultimate reality."[10] Consequently, we can imagine God emanating grace and love like a celestial beacon. As these hallowed waves are ever-present and accessible, we attune our spirits through practices of piety to receive the sacred signal.

For Cynthia Bourgeault, the spirit's mechanism of divine reception is the heart. She shares an age-old understanding that the heart is the location of the "spiritualized mind," an "organ of spiritual perception."[11] Bourgeault captures the essential role that our core being plays in the spiritual drama using the words of the modern Islamic mystic Kabir Helminski:

> *Beyond the limited analytic intellect* is a vast realm of mind that includes psychic and extrasensory abilities;

intuition; wisdom; *a sense of unity*; aesthetic, qualitative and creative faculties; and image-forming and symbolic capacities. Though these faculties are many, we give them a single name with some justification for they are working best when they are in concert. *They comprise a mind*, moreover, *in spontaneous connection to the cosmic mind. This total mind we call "heart"* (emphasis added).[12]

This concept of the "heart/mind," then, as the seat of our true selves, is critical to our interaction with divine grace. Returning to our signaling metaphor, maximizing the heart's input from the sacred font implies an optimal position or orientation. Bourgeault's concept of "nondual consciousness" represents the heart in its most receptive state (receiving "pure signal"), and its attainment is central to her philosophical outlook. Exploring this idea further brings us closer to our definition of unitive perception.

Bourgeault defines "dualism" as a subject/object posturing. As subjects, we typically reflect on or consider some object that we deem "external" to ourselves. This analytical mode of perception creates a de facto partition or separation between the subjective "I" and the objective "it."[13] Even our language constructs reinforce this perception. For example, English grammar typically follows the subject/verb/object (SVO) construction. Subjects have agency, operating on the object via the action described by the verb. The language does not inhibit our reception, per se, but it does frame what we see.[14] From this model, no matter how we try to change what we observe, the partition remains.

By contrast, a nondual-consciousness approach shifts the paradigm altogether. Instead of attempting to change *what* we see—changing the *object* of perception—nonduality concerns itself with changing *how* we see—the *mode* of perception. No longer do we perceive a dog as "merely" a four-legged creature of a certain color and breed, having to be fed and house-trained. Instead, we understand it as a fellow participant in creation, complete with feelings, experiences, and God-given purpose like our own. Bourgeault refers to this type of acuity as "heart-centered cognition."[15]

The notion of heart-centered cognition rests in holistic reception, allowing ourselves to come into "sympathetic resonance" with our environs. The differentiating mind takes a back seat to the mind's parallel processes that tend to receive more broadly.[16] By harmonizing or sympathizing with the experiences we receive, we open ourselves to an intimacy with all creation. Consider, for example, this seemingly common experience:

> When we are in the field of the heart, we are in the flow and void of resistance. We are in a space of grace, where anything can happen, and where nothing takes time because everything is available to us instantly through the eternal-now.... [Consider] the experience of meeting someone for the first time and connecting so totally heart-to-heart that it feels like you have known them for years, or all your life, or even forever, when in fact, in linear time, you have known them for only a few moments.[17]

Such synchronicity is a natural by-product of the shift from "thinking" with our heads to "experiencing" with our hearts, the part of our existence that is blessed to have contact with the Divine. And it is that holy communication that lies at the root of unitive perception. Its sacred purpose resides in our understanding of our place in creation and connectedness to it, a comprehension that demands an appreciation of our unified participation in the life of the One through Christ: "*As you,*

Father, are in me and I am in you, may they also be in us..." (John 17:21; emphasis added). As Bourgeault aptly states, "[We] see oneness because [we] see *from* oneness."[18] Our definition is the synthesis of these ideas.

Unitive perception is the means of seeing holistically, resisting the natural tendency for our divisive brain to dominate, but deferring to that part of us that takes in the whole. It embraces Bourgeault's idea of heart-centered cognition, which enables nondualistic consciousness while maintaining its sole identity and purpose as the participation in God through the "mind of Christ."[19]

Digesting these ideas, we must admit that fundamentally shifting how we see the world is no walk in the park. As we have noted, moving from the "head to the heart" runs counter to our cultural experience, including even the language we speak. It suggests a level of reprogramming how we receive the world— a "re-wiring" of our mental and spiritual circuitry—that implies work on our part. This effort, as with all attempts at change, begins with prayer.

The fourth-century monk Evagrius Ponticus provides sage guidance in his *Chapters on Prayer*, a manual intended to aid his fellow monastics on their spiritual journey):

> The Holy Spirit takes compassion on our weakness, and though we are impure he often comes to visit us. If he should find our spirit praying to him out of love for the truth he then descends upon it and dispels the whole army of thoughts and reasonings that beset it. And too he urges it on the works of spiritual prayer.[20]

The course of change begins with the help of the Spirit through prayer. We implore God to impart the grace we need to persevere, knowing that, while grace is sufficient, we nevertheless maintain a role in this synergistic relationship. And as we engage in our work, Evagrius's wisdom proves timeless. As we seek solace and even answers through prayer, the discipline of prayer *itself* provides a solution.

CONTEMPLATIVE PRAYER

The *Westminster Dictionary of Theological Terms* defines monotheistic prayer as a "human approach to God and addressing God in praise and adoration, confession, thanksgiving, supplication, and intercession."[21] This entry is ostensibly consistent with the categories we laid out in the introduction that resonate with Paul's understanding in his First Letter to Timothy where he urges that "supplications, prayers, intercessions, and thanksgivings be made for everyone" (1 Tim 2:1). While these rudimentary categories of prayer suffice, their two-dimensionality leaves us flat and needing more. Our lives suggest that "prayer" is enmeshed with the rudiments of human experience.

One expansive yet somewhat common view of prayer is that it is about conversation with God. By its nature, such a view suggests a two-sided sharing of ideas, an implied mutuality. This reciprocal nature of prayer is found in the Psalter. Its pages reveal God as "a full participant in a life of lively dialogue," and one who prays is a partner in that conversation, "capable of being an *initiator* or a *respondent*" in the exchange.[22] Adding more nuance, prayerful speech is nothing less than "the exchange of thoughts *and of souls, unity in a common spirit*, in a common possession and sharing of the truth" (emphasis added).[23] However, recognizing that—given the nature of its participants—this mutuality is uneven in its distribution, we must quickly qualify this human/divine interaction. We temper all such ideas by noting that "prayer is a conversation in which

God's word has the initiative and we, for the moment, can be nothing more than *listeners*. Essentially, we *hear God's word and discover from it how to respond...*" (emphasis added).[24] This ability to listen, this demand for silence in the Divine Presence, is our call to contemplation.

Contemplation is an act of inner awareness. James mentions those who, after gazing upon themselves in a mirror, immediately "forget what they were like" once they turn away from it (Jas 1:23–24). As already noted, the spirit is that place where the Divine speaks to us, guides us, and creates relationship with us. It is home to our true nature, and it longs for intimacy with God. James here suggests that we need to participate in the Word to remember who we are called to be. The intentional activity of spiritual awareness through contemplation assists us in being mindful of our true selves. But before we advance, we should take a moment to consider those modern voices that may object to this mode of spiritual discipline.

Two streams of thought oppose the authenticity of Christian contemplation. The first situates contemplation in the "New Age" movement, a modern adaptation of earlier Asian so-called occult practices. The core offense, here, is the idea of attaining an altered consciousness or other state with the aim of "getting Christ," not unlike the self-realization methods of Hinduism or Buddhism as popularly understood. At the very root of this resistance, though, is a rehashing of the age-old grace versus works argument.[25] The fourth-century Syrian monk Pseudo-Macarius, himself steeped in the tradition of interior prayer, refutes this misguided belief:

> Prayer produces among those who are worthy of it a certain mystical communion (*koinonia*) of holiness with God, *thanks to the action of the Spirit*. It brings about a certain union with the Lord that fills the human spirit

with an inexpressible love. And each day he who is moved to continue in prayer is drawn *by the love of the Spirit* to a love and a desire that is full of fire for God. Each one receives the grace from the Spirit of the perfection of a free will. *It is God who gives this gift* (emphasis added).[26]

The text resoundingly emphasizes that *any* attainment of connection with God originates with the Spirit. To use a sailing analogy: a sailor has no control over the wind (the Spirit). If the wind does not blow, the boat has no energy to move. However, if the sailor does not properly prepare—untie the knots, lift anchor, trim the sails, and tend the rudder—then, if by chance the wind does blow, the boat still will not move, or worse, it will launch haphazardly and without direction.[27] Contemplative prayer is the Christian's act of preparation to be at the full disposal of the Spirit.

The second stream of thought opposing the authenticity of Christian contemplation is that contemplation resonates only within the Roman Catholic tradition. One representative of this camp argues that the end state of prayer is being in the will of God, "not the contemplation of his being."[28] The record consistently shows that the end state of contemplation is not so much "being in God" as it is realizing God's kingdom as agents of compassion and grace, and the true aversion to this development of the inner life resides in the seemingly incompatible Roman and Protestant theologies of grace.[29] Since the purpose of this text is not to offer an apology for either of these positions, we instead offer an anecdotal example that points to the contemplative life as alive and well in the history of Protestant thought. While there are numerous treatises that combat the idea of contemplation's absence from the various branches of Christianity (Protestantism is not monolithic in its expressions), one robust excerpt from the memoirs of the eighteenth-century Congregationalist Jonathan Edwards serves to buttress the counterargument:

> Once, as I rode out into the woods for my health, in 1737, having alighted from my horse in a retired place, as my manner commonly has been, to walk for divine contemplation and prayer, I had a view, that for me was extraordinary, of the glory of the Son of God, as Mediator between God and man, and his wonderful, great, full, pure and sweet grace and love, and meek and gentle condescension. This grace that appeared so calm and sweet, appeared also great above the heavens. The person of Christ appeared ineffably excellent, with an excellency great enough to swallow up all thought and conception—which continued, as near as I can judge, about an hour; which kept me the greater part of the time in a flood of tears, and weeping aloud. I felt an ardency of soul to be, what I know not otherwise how to express, emptied and annihilated; to lie in the dust, and to be full of Christ alone; to love him with a holy and pure love; to trust in him; to live upon him; to serve and follow him; and to be perfectly sanctified and made pure, with a divine and heavenly purity. I have several other times had views very much of the same nature, and which have had the same effects.[30]

Edwards's account is congruent with the reports of his Roman Catholic (and Orthodox) counterparts. It presents the idea that contemplation is consistent with the history of Protestant thought (in Edwards's case, Calvinistic) and experience, and it illustrates and strengthens the argument for what Christian contemplation truly is—an emptiness before God to attend to the fullness of God's grace in Christ, void of doctrinal dogmas or arguments. Let us now trace the path of Christian contemplation as it was preserved most reliably.

The notion of contemplation has been nurtured most conspicuously in monastic practice. In the sixth century, Benedict of Nursia synthesized Eastern and Western monastic practices through the creation of his Rule. In chapter 6 of the Rule, Benedict sets the contemplative tone, dictating that "the master should speak and teach, and the disciple should quietly listen and learn."[31] The twelfth-century Cistercian monk Bernard of Clairvaux mentions in his seventh parable what by that time was a known formulary, the "precious fabrics" of "readings, meditations, prayers, and contemplations."[32] And in his *Sayings of Light and Love*, the sixteenth-century Carmelite mystic John of the Cross plays upon Jesus's teachings (cf. Matt 7:7; Luke 11:9) and that same fourfold structure: "Seek in *reading* and you will find in *meditation*; knock in *prayer* and it will be opened to you in *contemplation*" (emphasis added).[33] While these categories historically represent the stages of biblical prayer known as *lectio divina* ("divine reading"), we will analyze these four classes of *lectio* (reading), *meditatio* (meditation), *oratio* (prayer), and *contemplatio* (contemplation) to understand different practices that collectively we term contemplation.

The term *lectio* translates as "reading." The ancients, of course, understood scripture (and Christ) as God's revelation, and therefore the study of written materials was paramount. Their understanding, however, moved beyond the literal understanding of "reading" to include listening to biblical and spiritual words and memorizing them. In fact, *any* means of receiving divine revelation rested within this purview; the emphasis was on *reception*.[34] Anything perceived (read) "spiritually" reveals a lesson.[35]

Not only must we receive these divine gifts, we must also completely own them. *Meditatio*, or meditation, involves this appropriation. Unlike the term's common use in Asian religious traditions, Christian meditation presumes an active and continual processing of revelation.[36] This processing may include repetitive speech, imaginative engagement, or some other means by which the mind remains affixed to its sacred cause. The mind is intentionally engaged, mulling over its subject until this type of prayer becomes "second nature." The analogy of a cow chewing its cud supplies an ancient yet wholly adequate image: the animal repeatedly gnaws and grinds, and as the food courses through the cow's digestive system, a fermentation process deep within extracts all the nutrients. The by-product is a "rich, creamy milk—a symbol of love filled with the unction of the Holy Spirit."[37] Like Jacob wrestling on the banks of the Jabbok, the one in meditation refuses to release the hallowed catch until it relents with a blessing.

The response to the blessing of meditation is *oratio*—prayer. This response comes from the penetrating awareness of God's reality. It moves. It provokes. It refuses to be ignored, and the one who prays is compelled to answer its call. The spirit splashes in the waves of divine awareness, the expanse and the refreshment of the waters evoking an uncontrollable outpouring. There may be shouts of praise; there could be cries of lament. Whatever the prayer, its release is inevitable. Eventually, however, the *activity* of prayer all but ceases. A joyful weariness sets in, and the soul begins to submerge. But this is no drowning. Like a mammal that suddenly sprouts gills, the soul adapts naturally, breathing in the totality of its spiritual environs.

Once immersed in the consecrated pool of divine experience, the soul is no longer aware of its expressions. Words are not spoken because the ideas they attempt to express are not applicable here. Consciousness has shifted to a boundless space, and linear time halts. All that remains is the water, itself the Spirit that is known only as the All in All. These are the ineffable depths of *contemplatio*. Alone with the Presence, nurtured by silence at the deepest level of contemplation, one experiences a quiet but profound encounter with the Living God.

Understanding the nuance of each segment of *lectio divina*, we can now appreciate the affinity between each of its phases and various prayer practices. Praying the Psalms, hearing the stories of inspirational figures, or even strolling through nature potentially provides the raw material for *lectio* or "reading." When such activities are carried out with prayerful intent, the Spirit may unexpectedly open us to receive revelatory splendor. Practices such as repeatedly reciting the "Jesus Prayer"—"Lord Jesus Christ, Son of God, have mercy on me, a sinner"—or immersing ourselves in imaginative engagement with scriptural scenes and/or characters resonate with the movements of *meditatio*. Christian meditation implies an active and conscious use of the mental faculties in pursuing God. Meanwhile, entering a conversation with God as our "Holy Therapist" as we reflect deeply on the day's activities and interactions would exemplify *oratio*. Methods such as the multi-faceted *Examen* embody this type of introspective engagement, a self-exposure that can be so deeply intimate as to inevitably result in praise and/or lament.[38] Lastly, the practice of Centering Prayer aptly illustrates the wordless engagement of *contemplatio*. This form of prayer demands intentional stillness and solitude, with an eye toward diminishing "self" by ignoring internal distractions and creating space for the Spirit to speak and be heard. All these are but a sampling of prayer forms that we might unconsciously engage in daily. While we may or may not know their "technical" designations, our spirits nevertheless are moved by them.

Like a greeting card, the words of another can sometimes capture a sentiment so well and so succinctly that we let them speak on our behalf. In defining contemplative prayer, David Keller writes that contemplation is "a grace-filled attentiveness to God that initiates and sustains a change of consciousness, leading to deepening love of God and neighbor."[39] It is this definition that we will use in this book.

CONCLUSION

Before moving on to the next chapter, let us consider briefly one of the forebears of contemplative prayer, Origen of Alexandria (185–254). Origen represents the early stages of Christian thought. He and his contemporaries equated seeing God with faithful discipleship, faithfulness modeled in the biblical text. One of Origen's greatest achievements involved the interpretation of scripture. He believed that understanding of the sacred text flows from a literal to a mystical interpretation, which is accessible only via "the movements of prayer," contemplative actions that condition us for God's revelation.[40] Following Origen's lead, we begin our study of the role of contemplative prayer in Christian unitive vision by turning to scripture.

2

Unitive Perception, Contemplation, and the Bible

Near the completion of the pastor's study on prayer, one of the participants approached him on a Sunday morning. She wanted to assure the pastor that she was attempting to maintain the practice as he had prescribed, and she added that upon conclusion of the study, she intended to continue her contemplative work. She would "continue seeking," determined to penetrate the mysterious depths of prayer in this fashion. She intimated that at the heart of her zeal lay the profundity of her encounters with scripture. While many of her daily readings still left her perplexed, she nevertheless was experiencing newfound clarity and insight from the scriptural texts. Something about the Bible's message was resonating with her contemplative prayers.

Contemplative prayer evolved from the ancient Christian practices that became known as "mysticism." The late Evelyn Underhill, a preeminent scholar in this field, defined mysticism as "that organic process which involves . . . establishing [a person's] conscious relation with the Absolute."[1] For Christians, this process was originally rooted in the interpretation of scripture, specifically through the use of a multi-layered approach. In the third century, Origen was a preeminent exemplar of this type of approach, distinguishing between a surface-level reading of the text that any literate person could appreciate and a deeper rendering of the message that "escapes the notice of most." Origen considered scriptural writings so shrouded in mystery that their meanings would be availed only to those "on whom the grace of the Holy Spirit is bestowed in the world of wisdom and knowledge."[2] Later theologians followed his lead.[3]

It was the sixth-century writer Pseudo-Dionysius the Areopagite who coined the term "mystical theology," so named after one of his brief treatises on the topic. In that work, he too alludes to the greatest depths of biblical insight, prefacing his essay with a prayer that God would lead the faithful "up beyond unknowing and light, up to the farthest, highest peak of *mystic scripture*, where the mysteries of God's Word lie simple, absolute and unchangeable in the brilliant darkness of a *hidden silence* (emphasis added)."[4] This tendency to view the sacred texts as the primary means of contemplating the mystery of the Divine lasted through the Middle Ages, with the Bible as the central object around which "reading, meditating, preaching, and teaching" maintained their orbits.[5] However, those in the early church viewed the Bible as more than a *means* to divine consciousness; they also understood its sacred pages as *instructional* to the purpose and practice of contemplation.

Early theologians excavated the recesses of scriptural mines searching for gems that would inform their daily spiritual walk, often emerging with treasure of immeasurable worth. One such find appears in the passage in 2 Corinthians 3:17–18. The word in verse 18 that the NRSV translates as "reflected" (*kataptrizomenoi*) was often interpreted by early church scholars as "contemplating." As such, these verses became the basis for the historical understanding that perfecting the image of God that we all carry within ourselves—the *purpose* of contemplation— was in part facilitated by reflecting upon Christ—the *practice* of contemplation.[6] Thus, the scriptural pages themselves served as the fertile soil for contemplative prayer, a means of grace by which the Christian could cultivate his or her call to holiness. This interpretation maintains its luster today.

Like the treasure-hunters of old, we too probe the hallowed grounds of scripture to find precious nuggets that mark this same purpose and practice. This chapter explores scripture to see how *the Bible richly informs our implied goal of unitive perception and* the proposed vehicle to that end, *contemplative practice.* By examining pertinent texts throughout the canon, we will understand how viewing the world holistically relates to the idea of unity through Christ, and we will better appreciate the "grace-filled attentiveness to God" (contemplation) as a means of aligning to the divine will of loving God and neighbor.

THE BIBLE AND UNITIVE PERCEPTION

Before examining contemplation's practice and purpose, we should first call our attention to unitive perception as a worthwhile biblical cause. In his 1934 work "Choruses from the 'Rock,'" poet T. S. Eliot penned these words: "What life have you if you have not life together? There is no life that is not in community, [and] no community not lived in praise of [God]."[7] Religious academics have used Eliot's sage declaration and applied it to the theme of unity in the Letter to the Ephesians, specifically 4:1–16. One such scholar notes that the church "unites with the *mission of God to unite all things,* things in heaven and things upon earth, that is, to bring the whole creation into *harmony to the praise and glory of the creator*" (emphasis added).[8] These holistic views of unity for God's purposes hit the mark.

The concept of "unity" in Ephesians is reinforced by Paul's use of the term in verses 4:3 and 13. The word's Greek root reveals a straightforward interpretation, describing a "bond of unity" that is especially manifested by God between believers.[9] While the only appearances of "unity" in the entirety of the canon occur in this letter, its meaning nevertheless captures the spirit of wholeness communicated throughout scripture. It is a constant theme of the faithful being *united by God, in Christ,* and *through the power of the Spirit.* Through this harmony, the people *live with a single mind and purpose,* lacking discernable division relating to the common goal. It is not integrity for its own sake, however; rather, it is a state that *mirrors the glory of the unified life within the Godhead,* a life in which we are invited to participate. Textual evidence for each of these claims suggests the authors desired their audiences to share in this vision of unity.

United by God

From the time of the patriarchs, the biblical record attests to the idea of God choosing and unifying a people to fulfill the divine purpose. As early as the calling of Abraham, God's words in Genesis speak to this truth: "*I* will make of you a great nation, and *I* will bless you, and make your name great, so that you will be a blessing. *I* will bless those who bless you, and the one who curses you *I* will curse; and in you all the families of the earth shall be blessed" (Gen 12:2–3; emphasis added). Likewise, during Moses's commissioning as an agent of Israel's delivery from Egypt, God instructs him to tell the assembly, "*I* will take *you* as *my* people, and *I* will be *your* God" (Exod 6:7; emphasis added). As with Abraham, God is clearly the primary actor. However, the notion of chosenness has expanded—now the "you" and the "your" are plural in their implications. Nevertheless, God sees the people as an integrated whole and looks to instill within them that same vision of solidarity based upon their common deliverance. A survey of the broader text reveals this same pattern.

The Hebrew Bible is replete with further examples of the people being reminded of their unity as God's possession. Passages like "The LORD your God has chosen you" (Deut 7:6) and the "people whom you have chosen" (1 Kgs 3:8) allude to an assembly of the faithful set apart by God. Through the prophets Isaiah and Ezekiel, God speaks in personal terms: "I have called you by name, you are mine" (Isa 43:1) and "on the day when I chose Israel...I swore to them, saying, I am the LORD your God" (Ezek 20:5). Still other samples promote a deep, familial intimacy, as in Malachi's cry, "Have we not all one father?" (Mal 2:10), and Hosea's beautiful poetry, "When Israel was a child, I loved him, and out of Egypt I called my son" (Hos 11:1). Resonating with this imagery, we can envision the entire biblical canon taking a form that identifies the faithful as "[embracing] the call and [believing] the promise," a people seeing themselves as explicitly shaped by God into a single "family."[10]

The New Testament writers continue with this vision of Godly kinship. In John's Gospel, the high priest Caiaphas is said to "prophesy" Jesus's death, a death that the narrator tells the audience would "gather into one the dispersed children of God" (John 11:52). The common bond between these "children" is their true Father, who, according to Jesus, is the "one in heaven" (Matt 23:9). In the Letter to the Ephesians, Paul reiterates the source of this spiritual paternity, noting that there is "one God and Father of all, who is above all and through all and in all" (Eph 4:6). Paul also notes that it is only by God's "enabling" that any can "share in the inheritance of the saints" (Col 1:12). And at the root of this enabling, of course, is the "spirit of adoption," the overall joy of which compels the faithful to see each other as integral parts of a greater whole, and to cry out to God in the most endearing of terms, "'Abba! Father!'" (Rom 8:15).

Paul notes that through this holy covenant, the faithful are counted as "God's own people" (Eph 1:14). This phrase appears in only one other book in the New Testament, where the author pronounces boldly to his Christian audience, "But you are a chosen race, a royal priesthood, a holy nation, God's own people"

(1 Pet 2:9). While this short passage is rich in allusions to God's calling of Israel in Exodus and Isaiah, focusing briefly on the words "nation" and "people" informs our discussion. The word translated as "nation" in this passage from 1 Peter is *ethnos*, from which we get our term "ethnic."[11] Given the diversity of cultural backgrounds from which 1 Peter's audience would have emerged, applying the term *ethnos* to the faithful most likely "gave them a sense of common identity" in an otherwise divisive context; now they were empowered to perceive themselves through the lens of solidarity and common cause.[12] A second word of interest may have had a similar effect.

The term *laos* or "people" appears over fifteen hundred times in the Hebrew Bible, with most instances referring specifically to the "people *of God*." Once again, the author of 1 Peter appropriates this word from the Judaic lexicon and applies it to his Christian audience. His reasoning is straightforward—as God elected the Israelites for the divine purpose, so too is the church set aside. Through God's adoption, individuals who once saw themselves as separate and distinct can now visualize themselves as *a* people, "chosen as [God's] heritage" (Ps 33:12). But that claim is valid only through the work of Christ.

In Christ

While the wholeness of the people is initiated and shaped by God, realizing that harmony is made possible in Christ. In John's Gospel, Jesus prays within earshot of his disciples, "The glory that you have given me *I have given them*, so that they may be one, as we are one" (John 17:22; emphasis added). Since Christ possesses the love *and* oneness of God as God's revelation, he is the only one capable of granting these divine gifts.[13] Additionally, some experts equate the "glory" bestowed by God on Christ with nothing less than the unfettered love that flows between the Father and the Son. This dynamic equivalence between God's glory and love suggests a foundational truth in that relationship—where this glory is present, so too exists a bond of loving and conspicuous unity. Working with that premise based on this passage of John, one scholar rightly comments, "Jesus prays that the oneness of love among believers might reflect the oneness of love that exists between the Father and the Son."[14] This same "oneness of love"—this impenetrable yet perceptible unity—is a golden thread deeply woven into the tapestry of the New Testament.

In fact, the entirety of chapter 17 of the Gospel of John represents Jesus's final prayer before his passion, and his intercession for unity is prominent throughout. As discussed, he highlights the Father's "glory" that he has imparted to his friends (v. 22). He prays for the disciples' "protection" through the divine name (v. 11). And Jesus petitions for "completeness" in their union with himself, the way of connecting with the Father (v. 23). All these prayers are to the end "that they may be one" (v. 22). Furthermore, these blessings are not limited to Jesus's immediate disciples; he opens his plea for unity to include all who come to believe through the witness of his immediate followers (vv. 20–21). Being gathered by Christ into "all that can be known of the reality of God" is the basis for this kind of unity, because that solidarity discernably imitates the oneness of Jesus and the Father.[15] A sampling of Paul's epistles reinforces this notion.

The theme of oneness in Christ is primary in Paul's letters.[16] When he addresses those baptized into the faith in Galatia, he aims to change how they perceive identity, insisting that neither ethnicity, servile status, nor gender has significance in their faith lives, "for all . . . are one in Christ Jesus" (Gal 3:28). Similarly, in a message to the Colossians the apostle plays down ostensible differences, promoting instead the view that "Christ is all and in all" (Col 3:11). Corresponding with the church in Ephesus, Paul speaks to the overt functions the "gifted" fulfill as the body of Christ, squarely focused on the unifying consummation of the faith "to the measure of the full stature of Christ" (Eph 4:11–13). He also makes use of this "body" metaphor to illustrate solidarity in his treatise to the Romans, writing that "we, who are many, are one body in Christ," and because of that relationship, "we are members one of another" (Rom 12:4–5; cf. 1 Cor 12:12–26). The corporal metaphor extends to the Eucharist; Paul compels the church in Corinth to recognize themselves in the sacrament: "[Because] there is one bread, we who are many are one body, for we all partake of the one bread" (1 Cor 10:17).[17]

Paul's eloquence in addressing the reconciliation of Jew and Gentile captures the idea of a palpable unity in Christ:

> But now *in Christ Jesus* you who once were far off have been *brought near by the blood of Christ*. For he is our peace; *in his flesh he has made both groups into one* and has broken down the dividing wall, that is, the hostility between us. He has abolished the law with its commandments and ordinances, *so that he might create in himself one new humanity* in place of the two, thus making peace, *and might reconcile both groups to God in one body through the cross*. (Eph 2:13–16; emphasis added)

This brilliant imagery sums up the work of Christ in bringing the faithful into oneness, both with himself and with each other. The reconciling power of love is the fire that forges this unity, and that love is no better revealed than through Christ's selfless act of the cross. This deed brings "access" to the Father, access quickened "in one Spirit" (Eph 2:18). A closer look at the activity of the Spirit reveals its unifying role.

Through the Spirit
Paul's letters sufficiently illustrate the certainty that we are united by God, in Christ, through the power of the Holy Spirit.

In Galatians, Paul enumerates for his audience nine different "fruits of the Spirit" (Gal 5:22). Among those listed, "peace" (*eirēnē*) appears early in the list. The "peace" referred to in that passage is literally a "harmony" among people, not far afield from the "wholeness" suggested by its Hebrew counterpart, *shalom.*[18] Therefore, when Paul implores the church at Ephesus to "[bear] with one another in love, making every effort to maintain the *unity of the Spirit* in the *bond of peace*" (Eph 4:2–3; emphasis added), he suggests that a visible byproduct of the presence of the Holy Spirit is the mutuality and unification of the faithful. That working assumption is directional for our premise when applied to other instances of Paul's work.

Paul understands the Holy Spirit as nothing less than the binding force of the community when he explicitly speaks of peace. In his view, when the mind is set on the Spirit, the outcome is "life and peace" (Rom 8:6). He sees the "power of the Holy Spirit" availing a wellspring of hope to "joyful and peaceful" believers (Rom 15:13). From Paul's perspective, the kingdom of God itself is identified by the "righteousness and peace and joy in the Holy Spirit" (Rom 14:17).

Even when the language of "peace" is absent, Paul still understands wholeness in the life of the community as an indicator of the activity of God's Spirit. When there is "sharing in the Spirit," the people are living "in full accord and of one mind" (Phil 2:1–2). As the giver of all good gifts, God's Spirit "activates" and "allots" talents that edify the body of believers "as the Spirit chooses" (1 Cor 12:4–11). Enriched by that grace, the collective lives of the people serve as a "letter of recommendation" for all to see, "written not with ink but with the Spirit of the Living God" (2 Cor 3:1–3). The rationale behind Paul's perspective is simple: through baptism, the faithful are integrated through the fellowship of the Spirit: "For in the one Spirit we were all baptized into one body—Jews or Greeks, slaves or free—and we were all made to drink of one Spirit" (1 Cor 12:13).

The "seven-fold unity" expressed in Ephesians 4:4–6 readily illustrates amalgamation through the Spirit. It makes plain that "oneness is a given, a truth over which we have no control. There is one body and one Spirit, one hope, one Lord, one faith, one baptism, one God and Father of all, a seven-fold oneness that should leave no doubt as to the significance of [this] affirmation."[19] The "peace" or "wholeness" alluded to here is inclusive of the Godhead ("Spirit . . . Lord . . . Father") as well as the "body" of the faithful. It reflects the glory within which we participate, the very depths of the Trinity, and we are called to bring it into view for others. To do so, we must first see ourselves as reconciled to oneness.

Singular Mind and Purpose

"The ministry of unity is a ministry of conciliation, which refers more generally to the process of bringing various different parties into relationships of mutual benefit and enrichment, in order to live in a model of unity. . . ."[20] This statement from the World Council of Churches in 2010 strongly endorses the purposes of seeing and realizing a corporate solidarity—attaining a singular mind and purpose that lacks division or any type of infighting. It is not a sense of uniformity; it is a clear eye on the common goal and the community's synchronized push toward that end. Paul has this ideal in mind as he writes to his congregations in Corinth and Philippi.

Learning of different "schisms" that have taken place in the Corinthian community, Paul appeals to his audience "that all of you should *be in agreement* and that there should be *no divisions* among you, but that you should be *united in the same mind and the same purpose*" (1 Cor 1:10; emphasis added). Paul is not concerned with "agreement" on minutiae here; the accord he seeks is a harmonious rhythm, a consecrated crew heeding the call of their spiritual coxswain toward the finish line. Likewise, sensing that some might be distracted by self-serving desires, Paul implores the church in Philippi to "be of the *same mind*, having the *same love*, being *in full accord* and *of one mind*" (Phil 2:2; emphasis added). His notion of unity is strongly conveyed, insisting on loving mutuality in purpose, and a twice-mentioned homogeneity of perception.

Paul, in fact, sees the unity of the church as imperative for the Christian and as a testament to the world. Once again addressing a Philippian audience, he states, "Only, live your life in a manner worthy of the gospel of Christ, so that, *whether I come and see you or am absent and hear about you, I will know that you are standing firm in one spirit, striving side by side with one mind* for the faith of the gospel..." (Phil 1:27; emphasis added). Paul seeks the community's oneness, not for self-affirmation but for the sake of the church and as a witness to the nations. Oneness "worthy of the gospel" is a sure sign that Christ is at the core of a community. It is proof that love is at work, binding the faithful and fueling their life as a whole. For the people of God, oneness must be experienced; it must be seen. What it mirrors is nothing less than God's oneness.

A Reflection of the Trinity

The entire Christian canon speaks to the uniqueness of God. This unity is expressed as resolutely today as it was when the *Shema* was first uttered: "Hear, O Israel: The LORD is our God, the LORD *alone*" (Deut 6:4; emphasis added). Similarly, Jesus recites this steadfast reality in Mark, removing any ambiguity as to the unitary nature of God: "'Hear, O Israel: the Lord our God, the Lord is *one*'" (Mark 12:29; emphasis added). However, both the Old and New Testaments strongly allude to distinct revelations of the personhood of God, such as the "spirit of God" in Isaiah (Isa 61:1; cf. 1 Sam 19:20; Job 33:4; Ezek 11:24), or the "Word" in John's Gospel (John 1:1, 14; cf. Rev 19:13). Even more overtly, Jesus commands the disciples to baptize "in the name of the Father and of the Son and of the Holy Spirit" (Matt 28:19), an explicit equivalency of the divine name, one which undoubt-edly calls into question the relationship between these revelations. Understanding that God is one, yet simultaneously recognizing that scripture unveiled something deeper within this unity, early Christians began pondering the "inner life" of God.

The eighth-century theologian John of Damascus wrote authoritatively about the relationship within the Trinity. His enduring words and concepts help to frame our discussion:

> The abiding and resting of the Persons in one another is not in such a manner that they coalesce or become confused, but, rather, so that they adhere to one another, for they are without interval between them and inseparable and their mutual indwelling is without confusion. For the Son is in the Father and the Spirit, and the Spirit is in the Father and the Son, and Father is in the Son and the Spirit, and there is no merging or blending or confusion. And there is one surge and one movement of the three Persons.[21]

The "mutual indwelling" of which John writes is known theologically as *perichoresis*, a term accredited to him because of this same passage. *Perichoresis* implies a circular dance of sorts, one in which it is hard to distinguish one swirling participant from another. The unity to which the people of God aspire is founded in this divine overlapping dance; the emulation of that same harmonious bond in love is their aim. Apart from God, human persons are unable to experience the depth of intimacy as does the Divine. However, the power of the Holy Spirit remedies this inability, "[indwelling] these separate subjects *and* [forming] a communion between them and a communion with them."[22] Given our divisive nature, harmony as a goal is out of reach without God. Yet through the work of the Divine, union within the body is not only possible, it is an expected truth among the faithful. And this reflection of the Trinity serves a purpose beyond the community itself; it manifests the glory of God. The canon attests to this truth.

From the outset, the chosenness of God's people served the purpose of pointing toward the Divine. This intent is somewhat veiled yet, nevertheless, apparent in Abraham's calling, when God informs him that his blessing is an instrument through which "all the families of the earth shall be blessed" (Gen 12:1). The world will readily see Abraham's progeny as set apart, a holiness that calls attention to the source of its sanctity. Upon the Israelites' release from bondage, this purpose is clearly stated: "I am the LORD who brought you up from the land of Egypt, to be your God; *you* shall be holy, for *I* am holy" (Lev 11:44–45; emphasis added). The church is under this same mandate.

As already noted, in the New Testament, the church is graced with sharing in the identity of "God's own people." Paul writes that participating in this inheritance is "to the praise of [God's] glory" (Eph 1:14). For the author of 1 Peter, membership in the unified household of faith is a privilege, but it simultaneously carries inherent evangelical responsibility: "that you may proclaim the mighty acts of him who called you" (1 Peter 2:9). This burden is a joyful task, and its ramifications are far-reaching.

Oneness in God is a reality toward which all of creation strives. The revelation of the Trinity provides the model of this unity, and God's chosen are called to emulate it. Stated differently but even more precisely, "the unity of God is for the unity of the church and the unity of the church is for the unity of the whole creation."[23] Solidarity is our purpose, and its achievement is emblematic of life in the kingdom. But as with all goals, this reality must be *perceived* before it can be *achieved*. The Spirit is the moving force behind this changed perception, and it follows that any tool that aids in receiving the Spirit ultimately assists in aligning the faithful with this divine understanding. Contemplation is just such a tool.

The Bible and Contemplative Prayer

Ignatius of Loyola was a sixteenth-century Spanish mystic who made important contributions to the contemplative tradition. His *Spiritual Exercises* provide several "annotations" that edify the reader in the use of his manual. In the first entry, he notes that just as "strolling, walking and running" are physical exercises, the prayer practices contained within the volume are analogues for "preparing and disposing the soul."[24] Much like Ignatius's systematic approach, the key to contemplation is *practice*, a definitive rigor applied to the faith in general, and to prayer life in particular, as a means of preparation (cf. 1 Cor 9:27).

The purpose or *function* of the practice is likewise well defined. If the goal is emulation of the "mind of Christ," then a basic assumption regarding the purpose of the discipline is our alignment with Christ's presumed perspective. The post-modern contemplative Ilia Delio describes this alignment as "[breaking] through our individual egos and [becoming] one with God in all our relationships so that, like Jesus, we create the world as reflection of the One we love, God."[25]

We will now explore the biblical record as it supports contemplation as a practice of preparation, and subsequently we will examine how this attitude of prayer parallels the mindfulness of Christ.

Quieting Self in Preparation

Contemplative prayer serves to prepare us to experience God. Like an orchestra that takes its tuning clues from the lead violinist, contemplation is a time of shutting off the distractions of the world to attune our hearts to the perfect pitch of the divine concertmaster. Known for her activity in the world, Saint Teresa of Calcutta appreciated the necessity of quiet and solitude in this fine-tuning process:

We too are called to withdraw at certain intervals into deeper *silence* and *aloneness* with God, together as a community as well as personally; to be *alone with Him*—not with our books, thoughts, and memories but completely stripped of everything—to dwell lovingly in His presence, *silent, empty, expectant, and motionless.* We cannot find God in noise or agitation (emphasis added).[26]

In this foundational instruction, Teresa highlights two key constituents of contemplative prayer—aloneness and silence. She also presumes a third element—or condition—that those who pray in solitude and quiet seek:

In the silence *of the heart* God speaks. If you face God in prayer and silence, God will speak to you. Then you will know that you are nothing. It is only when you realize your nothingness, your emptiness, that God can fill you with Himself. Souls of prayer are souls of great silence (emphasis added).[27]

Teresa presumes that the heart is the central "organ" toward which the practice of contemplation is targeted, and its purgation and conditioning are central to the experience of God. The contemplative foundations of *solitude, inner quiet,* and *purity of heart* are abundantly present in the scriptures.

In the Gospels, Jesus's deep, abiding prayer was facilitated by seclusion. In speaking of prayer he promoted isolation, instructing his followers to "go into your room and shut the door and pray" to God who "sees in secret" (Matt 6:6). He understood the value of solitude, and he withdrew often to engage in prayer. Sometimes he retreated to "deserted places" (Mark 1:35; Luke 5:16), while at other times he sought refuge in the "mountains," even through the course of the night (Luke 6:12; Matt 14:23; Mark 6:46). He occasionally shared the solitude with his disciples, as he did in Gethsemane (Matt 26:36; Mark 14:32; Luke 22:41). And in one instance of prayerful retreat, Peter, James, and John have a rare glimpse behind the veil, witnessing Jesus in the transfiguration (Luke 9:28–35; Matt 17:1–5; Mark 9:2–7).

Resonating with this notion of solitude, Delio writes, "Solitude is not being alone; it is being alone *with* God. It is not an escape from people but a deepening of one's heart in God so as *to be united with all that is of God.*"[28] Such solitude involves removing distractions—physical, psychological, or spiritual—to eliminate any background noise that may interfere with connecting with the Spirit of God. Contemplative prayer not only welcomes but prescribes this isolation. It is an environment that is conducive to cultivating and maintaining inner quiet.

John of the Cross wrote that the "Father spoke one Word, which was his Son, and this Word he speaks always in eternal silence, and in silence must it be heard by the soul."[29] As the prayer book of the Bible, the Book of Psalms sets the tone for this silence. The psalmist instructs those who pray to "ponder" and "be silent" when their souls despair (Ps 4:4). He compares the "quieted and calmed" soul to a weaned child, content to be in the arms of its mother (Ps 131:2). The faithful are not called to be anxious, but to "be still before the LORD, and wait patiently for him" (Ps 37:7). This stillness in prayer, as John of the Cross wisely assessed, is the prerequisite for receiving the Word: "Be still, and know that I am God" (Ps 46:10). It also creates an environment for discursive thoughtfulness on the things of God.

There are at least eighteen variations of the term "meditate" in the Book of Psalms as it relates to God or divine instruction. The first psalm sets the stage for the entire Psalter, describing as "happy" the disposition of those who meditate on God's law "day and night" (Ps 1:2). Meditation on the divine nature is central as the psalmist thinks of God on his bed "in the watches of the night" (Ps 63:6), or he moves from meditation to contemplation as his spirit "moans" and "faints" from the intimate contact (Ps 77:3). The theme of pondering the law is present in Psalm 119, the longest psalm in the Bible. It contains nearly 45 percent of all mentions of meditation, and over sixty-seven allusions to divine instruction. Biblical researchers have suggested that at some point in its development, the Psalter may have concluded with this entry.[30] In that context, Psalms 1 and 119 form "bookends" where meditation on God's precepts binds the life of prayer itself.

In Matthew, Jesus instructs his followers to "strive first for the kingdom of God and his righteousness" (Matt 6:33; cf. Luke 12:31), an admonishment to keep heaven's priorities front and center. Paul issues similar advice, penning to the church in Rome that "[setting] the mind on the Spirit is life and peace" (Rom 8:6). From this position of narrowly focused commitment, Jesus also encourages his disciples to "ask," "search," and "knock," understanding that inner purity of intent is rewarded from above (Matt 7:7; cf. Luke 11:9). Such authenticity originates from our essential core, or what Paul calls the "inmost self," the place that, like the psalmist, "[delights] in the law of God" (Rom 7:22). This center is the seat of our being, the confluence of our bodies, thoughts, emotions, perceptions, and even will.[31] It is the hushed location where we encounter God, often with silent "sighs too deep for words" (Rom 8:26). Jesus identifies this core as the "heart," the seat of our desires (Matt 6:21; Luke 12:34), and the depth from which our true self emerges (Luke 6:45). Contemplation is a means of purgation for the heart, "cardio" exercise that strengthens this organ of spiritual reception.

The contemplative pillars of solitude and inner quiet are grounded in scripture, and so too is the call for purity of heart. Psalm 24 responds to its own question: "Who shall ascend the hill of the LORD?" with an immediate and convicting answer: "Those who have clean hands and pure hearts" (Ps 24:3–4). In

Matthew, Jesus echoes this when he announces in his sixth beat-itude: "Blessed are the pure in heart, for they will see God" (Matt 5:8). Both passages present a case that "purity of heart" is a precondition for approaching the Divine. Through Ezekiel God also speaks of the heart, removing altogether the "heart of stone" and replacing it with one "of flesh" (Ezek 11:19; cf. 36:26), presumably renewed and open to divine interaction. Jeremiah, too, clarifies why purity of heart is so essential: it is to be the tablet of God's law, fresh clay inscribed directly from the instrument of God (Jer 31:33).

In its typical usage, the word "pure" (*katharos*) is synonymous with "clean," itself implying "being free from" persons or things (vis-à-vis, impurities).[32] As such, "purity of heart" ostensibly has something to do with removing those things that pollute our core selves. The twentieth-century mystic Henri Nouwen helps make the connection. In speaking of formation of the heart, he notes that "to let God's presence fill us takes constant prayer, and to move from our illusions and isolation back to that place in the heart where God continues to form us in the likeness of Christ takes time and attention."[33] Quiet contemplation serves as this type of preparatory prayer.

As Paul built a case to the church at Galatia regarding justification by faith, he made a profound observation. In his Letter to the Galatians, Paul fully understood the transformation into the "likeness of Christ" to which Nouwen alludes. Because of his own transformation "in Christ," Paul could boldly proclaim, "It is no longer I who live, but it is Christ who lives in me" (Gal 2:20). Looking inward, he saw the heart of Christ—the living law imprinted on his core being. That same Christ-like perspective translated to his view of the world.

Aligning with Christ's Perspective

The Bible not only endorses the *practice* of cultivating the inner silence of contemplation, it also aligns with the *purposes* of that practice. Delio wonderfully articulates the pragmatic side of this reality, noting that "gospel life is *praxis*; it begins with *awareness of God's presence and discernment of the inner mind or spirit. It is a life of awareness* that something new is being formed and an invitation to be part of the creative process" (emphasis added). She also understands the ultimate function or purpose of this connectional practice:

> Thus, Christian life requires a conscious decision to shift the mind (*metanoia*) by training the mind *to focus on the central values of the gospel and to dispense with all other things.* Without the choice for a new level of consciousness, there can be no new reality or reign of God. Where our minds focus, there our treasure lies (emphasis added).[34]

Focusing on "the central values of the gospel" implies aligning our values to those of Christ. It means a "shift" in our perspective to one that replicates Christ's teachings and actions. With this divine pattern as our guide, we will now explore how scripture endorses contemplation's function of perfecting the image of God within ourselves as an act of seeking, as an act of humility/selflessness, and as an act of unification.

Contemplative prayer is an act of seeking God, an entreaty by Jesus (cf. Matt 7:7; Luke 11:9) that is endorsed throughout the canon. Some of these endorsements involve indirect appeals. Before they cross into the land of promise, Moses prophesies that the people will "seek the LORD your God, and you will find him if you search after him with all your heart and soul" (Deut 4:29). David's psalm of thanksgiving before the ark entreats the faithful to "[seek] the LORD and his strength, seek his presence continually" (1 Chr 16:11). Likewise, the psalmist expresses an inner desire to seek out God, exclaiming, "'Come,' my heart says, 'seek his face!' Your face, LORD, do I seek" (Ps 27:8). Paul echoes this wisdom, linking the pursuit of God with true perception: "There is no one who has understanding, there is no one who seeks God" (Rom 3:11; cf. Ps 14:2). And the author of the Letter of James grounds this searching in pragmatic terms: "Draw near to God, and he will draw near to you" (Jas 4:8).

In other places, it is God who encourages the seeking. In Jeremiah, for example, God's words succinctly align with those of Christ: "When you search for me, you will find me" (Jer 29:13). Proverbs echoes this sentiment, but here God additionally affirms this pursuit as a loving act, stating, "I love those who love me, and those who seek me diligently find me" (Prov 8:17). The Chronicler, however, best presents the quest in unambiguous contemplative terms. Here, God declares that "if my people . . . *humble themselves*, *pray*, *seek my face*, and *turn* from their wicked ways, then I will hear from heaven . . ." (2 Chr 7:14; emphasis added). This notion of seeking God through humility in prayer to effect a change mirrors the work of Christ and strikes at the heart of contemplation.

Contemplation also promotes humility and selflessness, scriptural qualities wholly embodied by Christ. To be "selfless" implies an eradication of self-centeredness, where the "energy of self-will" is expended solely for self-gratification.[35] Such self-denial originates in humility, a submission to God that demonstrates the proper Creator/creature relationship. To that end, the prophetess Huldah declares to King Josiah through his agents, "Because your heart was penitent, and you humbled yourself before the LORD . . . I also have heard you, says the LORD" (2 Kgs 22:19). Likewise, Isaiah conveys God's preference for "the humble and contrite in spirit, who trembles at my word" (Isa 66:2). According to the psalmist, it is from this humble location that we are taught God's "way" (Ps 25:9). Humility is also expressed through John the Baptist's proclamation about Jesus, "He must increase, but I must decrease" (John 3:30); and ultimately, it is

depicted by Christ, who, foreseeing his own suffering, nevertheless utters, "not what I want but what you want" (Matt 26:39).
The contemplative adopts this same attitude, silently submitting
himself or herself to God's transformational power that enables
and delights in death to "self."

Jesus is the archetype of selflessness, giving himself up
completely for the sake of his "friends" (John 15:13). He
counseled his disciples that "if any want to become my followers, let them deny themselves and take up their cross and follow me" (Matt 16:24). In writing to the church at Ephesus,
Paul uses this theme of self-denial, interpreting our new
"death" to be that of the "old self." He reminds them: "You
were taught to put away your former way of life, your old self,
corrupt and deluded by its lusts" (Eph 4:22). His parallel between death and self-denial crystallizes in his nuanced address
to the faithful in Colossae:

> *Put to death*, therefore, whatever in you is earthly.
> ...These are the ways you also once followed, *when*
> *you were living that life*. But now you must *get rid of*
> *all such things*...seeing that you have *stripped off the*
> *old self* with its practices and have *clothed yourselves*
> *with the new self*, which is being renewed in knowledge
> according to the image of its creator. (Col 3:5, 7–10;
> emphasis added)

These verses (and others) describe a humility, a selflessness,
a denial of self that are central to the character of Christ and his
atoning work.

In Philippians, Paul describes Jesus's self-emptying action of
the cross. Again, the tight-knit relationship between humility
and selflessness is evident, the act of self-denial resulting in
physical death:

Let the same mind be in you that was in Christ Jesus, who, though he was in the form of God, *did not regard equality with God as something to be exploited*, but *emptied himself*, taking the form of a slave, being born in human likeness. And being found in human form, he *humbled himself* and became obedient to the point of death—even death on a cross. (Phil 2:5–8; emphasis added)

Christ evinces humility through taking human form, suffering, and dying, while his selflessness is displayed in the release or "emptying" of his divine right. Contemplative prayer emulates this same *kenosis*, releasing the inner conflicts and constructs of the "false self" and making room for the Spirit to claim its rightful ownership of the heart. The result is transformational.

Paul instructs his readers to "be transformed by the renewing of your minds, so that you may discern what is the will of God" (Rom 12:2). Contemplation is a process that can facilitate this renewal, disciplining the faithful to move beyond the limited ideas of themselves—positive or negative—to simply "be" in God, letting the Spirit indwell and work. Revisiting our reference to 2 Corinthians, we can better appreciate the early Christian grounding for contemplation:

Now the Lord is the Spirit, and *where the Spirit of the Lord is, there is freedom*. All of us, gazing [*contemplating*] with unveiled face on the glory of the Lord, *are being transformed into the same image* from glory to glory, as from the Lord who is the Spirit. (2 Cor 3:17–18; NAB, emphasis added)

These early contemplatives understood prayer as something that changed lives holistically, the Spirit transforming believers into their destined image—that of Christ. In this way the fire of the Spirit becomes a smelter of spiritual ore, purifying its subjects and recasting them as one Body.

Finally, contemplative prayer is an act of unity, the biblical task of aspiring to grasp the reality of the world and our connection to it as Christ perceives them, or "coming to see as the Spirit sees."[36] Jesus also had this vision. For example, when told that his "mothers and brothers" were waiting to speak with him, he responded, "Whoever does the will of my Father in heaven is my brother and sister and mother" (Matt 12:46–50; cf. Mark 3:31–35; Luke 8:20–21). Jesus was not scorning his relatives; his response was instructional on seeing with Christlike eyes—all are intimately related through God's love. In his Letter to the Romans, Paul confirms this relationality: "For those whom he foreknew he also predestined to be conformed to the image of his Son, in order that he might be the firstborn *within a large family*" (Rom 8:29; emphasis added). Jesus understood that, from heaven's perspective, the faithful are inseparably bound.

Paul directly experienced this same reality when he encountered Christ on the road to Damascus. Embedded in the question "Saul, Saul, why do you persecute me?" (Acts 9:4–5) is the implication that Paul's persecution of the church was an assault on Christ himself, a reality possible only if the two are mystically united. Paul confirms his lesson learned, penning that "anyone united to the Lord becomes one spirit with him" (1 Cor 6:17). Contemplation promotes receptivity to and comprehension of this unitive reality.

CONCLUSION

The thirteenth-century Rhineland mystic Meister Eckhart wrote, "The eye with which I see God is the same with which God sees me. My eye and God's eye is one eye, and one sight, and one knowledge, and one love."[37] This type of vision—seeing as God sees—is the crux of unitive perception. It is understanding that we are united by God, in Christ, through the power of the Holy Spirit, and this harmony of mind and spirit is nothing less than a reflection of the Divine Oneness. While this graced vision is imparted wholly by the Spirit, we are charged with preparation. Contemplation is such a preparation, paralleling the mindfulness of Christ in seeking God through humility and selflessness, with a keen eye on unity.

In his well-known letters to the Thessalonians, Paul counsels them to "pray without ceasing" (1 Thess 5:17; cf. Luke 18:1; Eph 6:18). To pray "constantly" moves beyond dedicated intervals of supplication; it means *living life* in a spirit of prayer, all thoughts, words, and deeds lifted as an offering to God. This is the mind of Christ, and Paul reminds us that to participate in that mind also includes participating "in the pattern of the cross," with the humility, suffering, and sacrifice that life entails.[38] While this is a seemingly daunting task, there have been those who have paved the way, demonstrating their attainment of unitive vision through a life of contemplation. It is to an example of these historical figures we now turn.

3

The Witness of a Mystic

Reflecting on the ninety-day period that made up the prayer "experiment," one of the participants shared her experience with the broader group of her fellow pray-ers: She had been arriving to work about thirty minutes earlier than normal, and, keeping the lights off in her office, she prayed through the contemplative curriculum that the pastor had outlined. About forty days into the program, a handful of her co-workers began to approach her individually to understand what she was up to. Parallel to the three-month prayer period, the participant's work environment was undergoing significant administrative changes, and the resulting uncertainty had created an atmosphere of stress and anxiety. The lone exception was this congregant. Her colleagues noticed her apparent sense of calm, and they understood her shift in demeanor to be related to her newly adopted ritual. Something about her very countenance had changed, and they wanted in on the secret.

Countless historical figures have chosen a life of contemplative prayer: Augustine, John Cassian, Bernard of Clairvaux, Hildegard of Bingen, Francis and Clare of Assisi, Bonaventure, Meister Eckhart, Julian of Norwich, John of the Cross, and Teresa of Avila are merely a handful of such luminaries. While their contributions vary due to time and context, they share a common bond of being classified as "mystics" in spiritual parlance. Recalling that Evelyn Underhill defined mysticism as a process by which we "consciously" connect with the Divine, this sacred connection is a natural result of "the embrace of [God's] unitive love."[1] Mystics are those who surrender to this embrace.

If contemplative prayer is foundational in forming a unitive perception of reality, then the witness of those who have dedicated themselves to engage in this deep spirituality should certainly buttress such an argument. In this chapter, we will examine a relatively obscure contemplative, Symeon the New Theologian, a medieval monastic representing the Eastern strand of the Christian tradition. Using his corpus as our source, we will (1) sketch a brief *biography* of his life, (2) *summarize three of his primary works* on contemplation, (3) examine his *ideas on and practices of contemplation*, and (4) present examples of his *attainment of unitive vision*. The portrait study will illustrate how contemplation contributed to Symeon's life, and particularly his perceptions. With this destination in mind, we point our attention eastward and chart a course toward the Byzantine world.

SYMEON THE NEW THEOLOGIAN

Born as George Galatones in Galatia, Asia Minor, this tenth- and early eleventh-century figure was born of nobility and had a culturally nurtured upbringing. The Byzantine spiritual atmosphere that surrounded Symeon had presumably become somewhat sterile and ritualized, catering to the institutional needs of the Empire over the spiritual concerns of the people. Additionally, an Eastern version of religious scholasticism was becoming the standard for discussion and practice, unnaturally deconstructing the symbiotic nature of doctrinal ideas *about* God and

the lived experience *of* God. After long bouts of prayer and reports of divine visions, Symeon felt compelled at the age of
twenty-seven to move from his world of patristic favors and
court appearances to monastic life.[2] As a monk, priest, and
eventually an abbot, Symeon sought to swing the theological
pendulum back toward experience.[3]

Several characteristics locate Symeon squarely within the
Eastern tradition. First, his title, the "Theologian"—assigned
upon his canonization—reveals that his teachings arose not simply from a brilliant intellect, but from a "deep mystical union
with God." In line with the idea of a theologian in the Eastern
context, Symeon would have considered any theological conversation "divorced from deep-seated belief and Christian experience" a "mockery of the concept of speaking about God."[4]
Second, he firmly embraced the idea of *deification*, a graceful
sanctification that has alternately been described as "a consciously experienced process of continued growth through intimate, loving communion with the Trinity."[5] Third, like his
mystical forebears Origen and others, Symeon primarily sought
God through biblical study. In "Discourse 24," Symeon compares scripture to a treasure chest whose contents exceed the
bounds of the imagination:

> Pay heed to me, brother, and apply this to spiritual
> things. Think of the chest as the Gospel of Christ and
> the other divine Scriptures. In them there is enclosed
> and sealed up eternal life together with the unutterable
> and eternal blessings which it contains, though unseen
> by physical eyes. As the Lord's word says, "Search the
> Scriptures, for in them is eternal life" *(Jn 5:39)*.[6]

Lastly, his ideas on prayerful encounters within and beyond
the biblical text set the tone for Gregory Palamas and others in
the tradition later known as *hesychasm*, a structured form of

"stillness" and "prayer of the heart" that serves as a mainstay of Orthodox spirituality today.[7]

Symeon's contemplative openness to the Spirit would determine the tone of his legacy. His sense of authority parallels that of the apostle Paul, legitimizing his teaching as direct knowledge from God. As such, he is known as a *theodidact*, one who is "taught by God."[8] Like Paul after his encounter with Christ on the road to Damascus (Acts 9:3–8) or his subsequent portage to the "third" heaven (2 Cor 12:2–5), Symeon reported an encounter with the "light" of Christ, even before his monastic career began in earnest:

> While he was standing in prayer one night, with his own pure intellect communing with the Prime Intellect, he suddenly saw a pure and immense light shining on him from the heavens above. Illuminating everything and making it bright as day. He too was illuminated by it, and it seemed that the whole building, along with the cell in which he was standing, vanished and all at once dissolved into nothingness, but he himself was *caught up* into the air and completely forgot about his body.[9]

Experiences like this convinced Symeon that divine revelation was not limited to the apostolic generation or to members of the magisterium who claimed it as their ecclesial right. Instead, anyone baptized into Christ could receive this spiritual gift and, in fact, given the right disposition toward God, should in fact expect it.[10] His works witness to these constants of his theology.

PRIMARY WORKS ON CONTEMPLATION

Before we examine Symeon's ideas on and practices of contemplative prayer, we pause momentarily to introduce the three key works that illustrate these ideas. Symeon's *Discourses* (aka *Cat-echesis*) is the seminal work of his years as the abbot of Saint Mamas.[11] These thirty-six installments represent written accounts of various daily sermons he delivered to his monks. The homilies enshrined his emphases on the themes of piety and the work of the Spirit, two critical foci which we will examine later in this chapter. In "Discourse 9," for example, Symeon instructs his audience on the virtues of giving to the poor:

> Cheerfulness consists in not regarding these things as our own, but as entrusted to us by God for the benefit of our fellow-servants. It consists in scattering them abroad generously with joy and magnanimity, not reluctantly or under compulsion *(cf. 2 Cor 9:7ff)*. Further, we ought cheerfully to empty ourselves of that which we stored up in the hope of the true promise God has made to us of giving us a hundredfold reward for this.[12]

For Symeon, acts of mercy represent an emptying of the self, a kenotic movement of charity that puts contemplative openness into action. And these are acts driven by the Spirit, the "key" of God's enlightenment of the human heart and mind, and the enabler of human movement toward God. Symeon reveals his pneumatologically based Trinitarianism in this excerpt from "Discourse 33":

> The Holy Ghost is spoken of as a key because through Him and in Him we are first enlightened in mind. We are purified and illuminated with the light of knowledge; we are baptized from on high and born anew *(cf. Jn. 3:3, 5)* and made into children of God.... This indicates to us that the door is light; the door shows us that He who dwells in the house is Himself unapproachable light *(1 Tim 6:16)*. He who dwells therein is no other

than God, His house is nothing else but light. Likewise the light of the Godhead and God are not two different things. He is one and the same, the house and He who dwells in it, just as the light and God are the same. In theological terms we use the term *house* of the Son, even as we use it of the Father, for He says, "Thou, O Father, art in Me, and I in them, and they in Me, and I, O Father, in Thee, that we may be One" *(cf. Jn. 17:21, 23)*. Similarly, the Spirit says, "I will live in them and move among them" *(2 Cor. 6:16)*.[13]

These two themes of devotion and the Spirit's shaping of the believer continuously emerge in Symeon's writings, underscoring his belief that the virtuous life is both an attempt to open to God and simultaneously a gift of the Spirit that empowers that effort. His second major work elaborates on these same dominant ideas in poetic meter.

During his tenure as abbot, Symeon also composed his *Hymns of Divine Love*. The fifty-eight entries that comprise this collection are marked by the intimacy we would expect from love poetry, complete with longing ("Let Your oil of grace drop, my God, and pour over my wounds"—"Hymn 46") and self-abasement ("I've shown myself worse than creatures without reason"—"Hymn 17"). Some are directly instructional ("Listen only to the advice of your spiritual father"—"Hymn 4"), while others read as prayers of thanksgiving ("I give thanks to You, Lord, I thank you, Unique One"—"Hymn 36"). Some passages are short ("Hymn 57" has 10 lines), while others are much longer ("Hymn 21" is more than 500 lines). Regardless of tone or length, the entire tome echoes Symeon's teachings and theologies, especially his lessons on devotion and the Spirit.

"Hymn 27" encapsulates examples of Symeon's constant shepherding in the ways of piety and his notions on the role the Holy Spirit plays in the believer's transformation. For example, he begins his poetic admonition: "Transform your soul into a place where Christ and King of all / may dwell by your flood of tears, your cries and lamentations, / by the bending of your knees and the number of your groanings, / if you truly, O monk, wish to be one who lives alone."[14] After a somewhat lengthy discussion of what this solitude in the Spirit is like, he ends with a return to the role of the virtues in aligning with the divine will:

> ... in the same way also everyone who seeks repentance
> and everyone who serves the Lord
> should strive also to be always with the preoccupation
> of how his repentance will be accepted
> and how his service will be pleasing and perfect.
> [And] then dwelling completely with God by means of
>   these virtues
> he is totally united and sees Him face to face
> and receives the child-like confidence to turn to Him
> in proportion that he hastens to accomplish his will.[15]

For Symeon, those who live the virtuous life are destined for the tears of penitence, a sacred solvent that cleanses the soul and hints at purity of heart. The ways of piety—of which contemplation is foundational—clear the clutter of misguided desires and superfluous points of focus; they create a space for God so that the believer "sees Him face to face." Despite human effort, however, conversion remains the sole domain of the Spirit. And when the Spirit is at work, the impact is undeniable.

The verses that follow in "Hymn 27" give us a clear view of Symeon's beliefs about the power of God's Spirit within:

> Do not say that it is impossible to receive the Divine
>   Spirit.
> Do not say without Him you can be saved.

47

Do not say, therefore, that one can possess Him without
    knowing it!
Do not say that God is not able to be seen by men.
Do not say that men do not see the divine light
or that this is impossible in these present times!
This is a thing never impossible, friends,
but on the contrary it is very possible to those who so
    wish,
but only to those who lead a life purified of the passions
and have purified, spiritual eyes.[16]

This hymn is emblematic of many of Symeon's writings and
thought. He rejects the notion that all cannot encounter the living Spirit, the sole saver of souls. He equally denounces the idea
that we can possess God's Spirit yet be unaware of it. For
Symeon, any who have achieved the appropriate amount of detachment from worldly desires are properly prepared to experience the Divine, their hearts purified and their "spiritual eyes"
opened by tears of repentance. And what they encounter is
nothing less than the Trinity indwelling within them.

   A third key resource comes in the form of a relatively obscure essay, "Practical and Theological Precepts" (hereafter
"Precepts").[17] This general treatise serves as an instructional
guide for Symeon's disciples after his resignation from the
monastery, providing counsel on ascetic and contemplative
practice. His dominant themes of piety and God's role in the
process are certainly present here, fully evident in statements
like, "it is right that we should ... bend our necks to the yoke of
Christ's commandments," or "without the fire of the Spirit,
everything he does will remain inactive and useless for his
aim."[18] The text is wholly concerned with the *approach* to contemplation. For example, Symeon counsels his audience that
"[our] mind is pure and simple, so when it is stripped of every

alien thought, it enters the pure, simple, divine light and becomes quite encompassed and hidden therein and can no more
meet there anything but the light in which it is."[19] Furthermore,
the essay reveals Symeon's understanding of the prayer life,
which we will address in more detail below.

Evagrius Ponticus outlined a two-tiered approach to contemplation, one of "nature"—including scripture, the cosmos,
and the natural order—and a second of the Triune God.[20] The
former was meant for contemplative adherents to consider their
natural surroundings prayerfully, including (and especially)
their own selves, while the latter was set aside until the faithful
achieved some mastery of the first. As we have already noted,
Symeon was solidly attuned to this tradition, and so we would
expect his ideas on the contemplative life to align with it. Since
Symeon's writings represent deep reflections on his *own* practice
and experience of God—as with any true "theologian" of his
time—close examination of some of these works provides a win-
dow into his world of contemplation. Continuing to use these
primary sources, we now need to determine Symeon's specific
conceptual and pragmatic engagement of contemplation as a
means of virtue, and subsequently, how that engagement framed
his perception of the Trinity.

SYMEON AND CONTEMPLATIVE PRAYER

In his "Precepts," Symeon comments that the person "who has
acquired *purity of heart* has conquered fear" (emphasis
added).[21] Later in that same text, he returns to and expands on
this topic of purity as it relates to penitence:

Mourning has a twofold action: like water *tears extin-
guish all the fire of passions* and *wash the soul clean* of

49

their foulness; and, again, through the presence of the Holy Spirit, it is like fire bringing life, warming and *inflaming the heart*, and inciting it to love and desire of God (emphasis added).[22]

To better understand Symeon's experiences, we specifically look at his attitudes toward the interrelated concepts of purity of heart, the "gift of tears," and detachment from the passions, also known as *apatheia*; all are central to this mystic's contemplative prayer life.

Purity of Heart

As we noted in the previous chapter, Jesus teaches the crowd in the Sermon on the Mount, "Blessed are the pure in heart, for they will see God" (Matt 5:8). Here, cleanliness of heart involves the purgation of impurities, creating and maintaining a personal "Holy of Holies" within which the Divine might dwell. Symeon provides his own working definition of this kind of purity, anchoring it solidly in a contemplative vision of blessing:

> *A heart is and is called pure* when it finds in itself no worldly thought, but wholly cleaves to God, and is so united with Him that it no longer remembers anything worldly, either sad or joyful, but *remains in contemplation*, soaring up to the third heaven, enters paradise and sees the blessings promised to the saints in their inheritance; and then accordingly it *reflects eternal blessings as far as is possible for human weakness* (emphasis added).[23]

Purity of the heart is an important goal for Symeon because the heart represents the "locus Dei," the "place of God" from which all spiritual connections originate.[24] Without purity, there is no ability to communicate with or experience God within.

Not surprisingly, then, the heart as a target of preparation and safekeeping is fundamental to Symeon's contemplative life. His pattern of prayer is primarily concerned with keeping the mind "in the heart." Situated there, the mind can experience the grace that nurtures the soul "as a hen gathers her chicks" (2 Ezra 1:30). "For by the sweet love of God the impulse of [the soul's] heart, or, rather, the whole inclination of its will, is bound. When once, as I have said, it has been bound to its Maker, how can it be inflamed by the body or in any way fulfill its own desires? In no way!"[25] Symeon's motivation for prayer is completely enmeshed in the symbiotic love between the heart and the divine source of its sustenance. This symbiosis is maintained by running "well in the practice of virtue," a race with Christ as its prize.[26]

For Symeon, the virtuous life is achieved by keeping the "commandments," and his writings evince that the commands to which he often alludes are not simply the Decalogue but are typically those encapsulated in Jesus's Sermon on the Mount.[27] In "Discourse 31," aptly titled "Self-Examination on the Beatitudes," the author moves through this series of sayings as a means of gauging personal piety. The sixth instruction on purity of heart (Matt 5:8) serves as a watershed for those that precede and those that follow. Symeon writes:

> Unless our soul attains to such a disposition [purity of heart] it can neither constantly *mourn* nor become perfectly *meek*, nor yet *thirst for God*, nor yet *become pure as a mirror*.... The soul, however, who has attained to this sees God from every (side) and is reconciled to Him.... Peace is established between our Maker and God on the one hand and the soul that was once hostile

to Him on the other, and it is then *called blessed by God for having made peace...* (emphasis added).[28]

Purity of heart is Symeon's key to fulfilling the virtues. And while he makes it very clear that the Holy Spirit is the agent through which all enlightenment is achieved ("virtues alone cannot make the heart pure without the action and presence of the Holy Spirit"), the primary means of preparing the heart for that Spirit is through the contemplative acts of self-examination and Christ-focus.[29]

There are two main components of Symeon's purgative prayer practice. The first consists of interior attentiveness. His younger contemporary and biographer, Niketas Stethatos, indicates that, prior to Symeon's tonsure, he received a book that spoke to the "examination of conscience." Taking this as divine instruction, Symeon began to do just that, and as a result his prayers lengthened at times until daybreak. Stethatos writes that it took but a few years for Symeon "to depart completely from what is visible and arrive at the invisible contemplation of God."[30] His routine often included retreats into solitude for up to three hours at a time, preparing himself "day by day to grow and bear fruit."[31]

For Symeon, the key to this form of prayer was discipline. In "Discourse 25" he notes that each of his colleagues needs to "fix in himself a standard and pattern" that, in turn, "keeps the ways in his heart."[32] Purification implies daily rigor and mindfulness of the inner self:

No less than the outward man, so must we needs adorn our inner man *(2 Cor 4:16)* with moderation of the Spirit, and completely offer up ourselves to God in soul and body.... By piety *(cf. 1 Tim 4:8)* we must *train the soul to think as it ought to think (Rom 12:3)* and *constantly meditate on the things that belong to eternal life*...and *by prayer invoke on itself the light of the Spirit*.... Apart from these not even its garment may ever be cleansed, let alone the *soul itself rise to the height of contemplation* (emphasis added except for scripture references).[33]

Maintaining this rigor shaped Symeon into the contemplative master that he was, girding him to offer prayers as a means of purgation. This excerpt from the lengthy "Hymn 17" poetically illustrates Symeon's experience:

I am seated in my cell / either by night or by day: / love is invisibly with me / and without my knowing it. / As it is exterior to all creatures, / it is also with them all; / it is fire, it is also ray, / it becomes a cloud of light, / it perfects itself as the sun. / Hence because it is fire, it warms the soul again / and burns my heart / and excites it towards desire / and love, love of the Creator. / And when I have been sufficiently inflamed / and set aflame in my soul, / like a ray carrier of light / it flies around and surrounds me entirely / casting its sparkling rays / into my soul, / illuminating my mind, / and it makes it capable / of the heights of contemplation / endowing it with a new outlook.[34]

The work for Symeon began explicitly with an inner focus and assessment. His openness allowed it to flower into a "new outlook," a changed perspective. Yet the object of his contemplative world remained steadfast.

The second component of Symeon's purgation of heart was his fixation on Christ. Mindfulness of the indwelling Christ is not an intellectual exercise, but is one wrought through contemplative consciousness.[35] He sets the trajectory for this contemplation in "Discourse 2":

Let us flee from the deceit of life and its supposed happiness and run to *Christ alone*, who is the Savior of
souls. Him let us endeavor to find who is present every-
where, and when we have found Him *let us hold Him
fast* and fall at His feet.... Nay, I entreat you, let us endeavor to *see Him and contemplate Him even in this
life* (emphasis added).[36]

Contemplation without Christ as its objective was completely foreign to Symeon, especially since it was the work of
Christ's Spirit that set the whole enterprise in motion. Pursuing
Christ either through a form of the Jesus Prayer or some other
centering means locked Symeon's intent onto its devotional
ends.[37] Even more specifically, it was the Christ-centered "light"
mysticism that Symeon clung to as his primary image, perma-
nently impacted by his first encounter as a young man. Using
Jesus's metaphor of the eye as the lamp of the body (cf. Luke
11:34), Symeon provides insight into the exegetical influences on
his prayer practice: "What else does He mean by 'the eye' than
simply the mind, which will never become simple unless it contemplates the simple light *(cf. Lk 11:34ff)*? The simple light is
Christ. So he who has His light shining in his mind is said to have
the mind of Christ *(1 Cor 2:16)*."[38] The mystic shares our understanding that putting on the "mind of Christ" is intricately entwined with the contemplation of the Triune God. His light motif
is a means of expressing a suprasensory experience that we understand as "deep calling on deep" (Ps 42:7), the wordless communication between created and Creator that is accommodated
only through the graceful economy of the Spirit. Nevertheless, he
attempts to articulate his "vision" through hymnody to encourage others to adopt and maintain the contemplative life:

Grant me, Christ, to kiss Your feet.
Grant me to embrace Your hands,

these hands which created me by Your word,
these hands which brought forth everything without effort.
Grant me to fill myself with these graces without being satisfied.
Grant me to see Your face, O Word,
and to enjoy your inexpressible beauty,
to contemplate and savor Your vision,
ineffable vision, invisible vision,
awesome vision; however, grant me to tell
not its essence but its operations.[39]

The rhythms of Symeon's christocentric prayer are like massaging fingers that ease the tensions of the heart, releasing its toxins and toning its structure for renewed strength in God. The inviting flow of the prayer's words beckon and encourage the listener to adopt this same pattern of contemplation, a preparation of our core being that opens us to new consciousness and horizons. Symeon issues these words from a place of intimate encounter, a state of purity that allows him the "privilege" of being directly taught by God.[40] And such an awesome gift demands great humility.

The Gift of Tears

Inseparable from Symeon's purity of the heart is the work of the Spirit that Evagrius termed the "gift of tears."[41] For Symeon, involuntary tears were an affirmation of contrition. The psalmist claims, "I am weary with my moaning; every night I flood my bed with tears; I drench my couch with my weeping" (Ps 6:6). Symeon promotes the same languishing position before God in penitence, an appropriate attitude of solemn compunction when approaching the Holy One in prayer. In "Hymn 17," he expresses this posture through heartfelt song: "Consider my teardrops / as ever gushing fountains, / O my Christ, / and wash my soul in them / from the stains of their passions."[42] The sacred waters of weeping are akin to the baptismal font, cleansing the soul and restoring the heart to its God-given image. In a clear parallel, Symeon explains that "[without] water it is impossible to wash a dirty garment clean, and without tears it is even more impossible to wash and cleanse the soul from pollution and stains."[43] He solidifies his argument for tears with a biblical appeal:

> No one will ever prove from the divine scriptures that any person ever was cleansed without tears and constant compunction. No one ever became holy or received the Holy Spirit, or had the vision of God or experienced His dwelling within himself, or ever had Him dwelling in his heart, without previous repentance and compunction and constant tears ever flowing as from a fountain.[44]

For Symeon, communication through contemplation requires the purgative power of tears. They are emblematic of the pray-er's contrition—a sign of the Spirit's movement in the human conscience. But this process is not one of complete sorrow. For Symeon, mourning has a "twofold action": the "first effect of mourning in God is humility; but later it brings unspeakable joy and gladness."[45]

For Symeon, tears were also an affirmation of joy. The psalmist holds firm to a hope that "those who sow in tears reap with shouts of joy" (Ps 126:5). Symeon's experience of contemplative tears has taught him likewise. In "Hymn 13," he expresses this spiritual irony:

> I weep, I am pierced with sorrow, when the light shines
>   on me,

that I see my poverty and that I realize where I am,
what world I live in, what mortal world, mortal myself;
and I am filled with joy, with bliss, when I understand
what condition God has bestowed upon me, what
   glory,
and I consider myself like an angel of the Lord
completely adorned with the immaterial garment.
Thus joy kindles my love for the Giver
and the One who transforms me, God—and
love causes streams of tears
to gush forth and makes me still more brilliant.[46]

Eyes and hearts flushed by tears of compunction are cleansed for a new vision, one that brings ineffable delight to the soul. That delight turns the bitter waters of contrition to sugar-sweet joy of divine revelation. With personal conviction Symeon can instruct his disciples that the penitential sorrow eventually "engenders increasing joy in our hearts and enables us to see the radiance that never sets."[47] Tears are tightly coupled with purity of heart, evidencing the contemplative's progression toward the things of heaven. That progression also requires detachment.

Detachment from the Passions

In Paul's letter to the church at Colossae, he offers the following advice on contemplation: "Set your minds on things that are above, not on things that are on earth, for you have died, and your life is hidden with Christ in God" (Col 3:2–3). The ancients interpreted this state as "impassibility" or *apatheia*, a condition of passionless existence—the calming of thoughts and desires that detract humanity from its truest purpose of pursuing God, a "re-integration of [our] whole being, senses, emotions, intellect and will."[48] *Apatheia* is a love-filled condition that "overcomes here and now...the wayward effects of disordered passion," liberating us to regain a sense of our created birthright.[49] This "overcoming" resonates with Symeon, for whom detachment is nothing less than a matter of human freedom. He notes that "a man whose thoughts are occupied with cares of this life is not free; for these cares hold him in their hands and make him their slave."[50] Reminiscent of Paul's dire appeal in Philippians against the "enemies of the cross of Christ" whose "minds are set on earthly things" (3:18–19), in "Hymn 15," Symeon issues a similarly solemn sentiment:

> But if you are clothed with the shamefulness of your
> flesh
> if you have not bared your mind, nor stripped your
> soul,
> if you have not succeeded in seeing the light,
> buried as you are in darkness, what could I really do for
> you,
> how should I show you the formidable mysteries?[51]

The mystic's outlook here is somewhat binary: For those who have "died in Christ" (Col 3:2–3), putting off the passions is symbolic of this death, a "white martyrdom" that raises the offering of self-denial in union with Christ's own self-giving.[52] Those who have not embraced this "enlightenment" remain "buried in darkness," blind to the mysteries of the faith. Those who do not let go of the cares of the world are like prisoners in a solitary confinement of their own creation. The keys of release are within arm's length, but the layers of attachments form deceptive lenses, like looking through the wrong end of binoculars. For the imprisoned, the mechanism of their freedom is perceived to be far off in the distance, completely inaccessible.

Evagrius wrote that the "soul which has *apatheia* is not simply the one which is not disturbed by changing events, but the one which remains unmoved at the memory of them as well."[53] Symeon, a spiritual descendant of Evagrius, adopted his teaching. He understood disordered passions as detrimental to sustaining a purity of heart, but he also believed that those no longer affected by them lived in a state he termed "supersensory"—completely attuned to God in love.[54] These blessed contemplatives have a renewed sense of reality, seeing things as they truly are—the world created through Christ (John 1:3; Col 1:16). One of Symeon's contemporary biographers summarizes this divine vision well: "Seeing a thing by the grace of the Holy Spirit with spiritual eyes 'according to the nature' means to go beyond the superficial impressions given us by our prejudiced faculties of knowing and judging through sense and emotional responses to outside stimuli."[55] This statement encapsulates our definition of unitive perception, a vision that was prominent in Symeon's life and work.

SYMEON AND UNITIVE PERCEPTION

Paul uses several metaphors to describe the faithful, such as "clothed in Christ" (Gal 3:27) and "children of light" (Eph 5:8). In "Discourse 28," Symeon applies both images to those who lack awareness of God's blessing of illumination, indicating that they will "appear naked" and be "filled with much shame."[56] Like the attendee without the proper garment at the divine wedding celebration (Matt 22:11–14), their absence of attentiveness will subject them to unwanted scrutiny. Symeon's accounts and biographical anecdotes indicate that through much contemplative struggle (purity of heart, tears, and impassibility) and the work of the Spirit, he had attained this consciousness. Two chief indicators of Symeon's unitive perception were his visions of light and awareness of the indwelling Trinity.

Visions of Light Motif
In his work *The Life of Moses*, contemplative and sage Gregory of Nyssa interprets the light emitted from the burning bush as nothing less than the light of God.[57] Symeon pays homage to his spiritual predecessor in "Hymn 23": "As Gregory / the Theologian has said: / illumination is the end / of all those who love; / and repose of all / contemplation is the Divine Light."[58] Symeon experienced this theophany of light firsthand on multiple occasions, and he not only recognized the significance of its occurrence, he also appreciated its transformational impact on how he would view the world thereafter. While he describes and/or alludes to several of these visions, two such experiences suffice to illustrate the transcendent nature of his encounter. In his first theophany, we can appreciate Symeon's struggle to articulate the scene:

> So I entered the place where I usually prayed and, mindful of the words of the holy man I began to say, "Holy God." At once I was so greatly moved to tears and loving desire for God that I would be unable to describe in words the joy and delight I then felt. I fell prostrate on the ground, and at once I saw, and behold, *a great light was immaterially shining on me* and seized hold of my whole mind and soul, so that I was struck with amazement at the unexpected marvel and I was, as it were, in ecstasy. Moreover, I forgot the place where I stood, who I was, and where.... *I conversed with this Light. The Light itself knows it*; it scattered whatever mist there was in my soul and cast out every earthly care.... Thus all the perceptions of my mind and my soul were wholly

concentrated on the *ineffable joy of that Light* (emphasis added).[59]

The profundity of this form of contemplation is indeed unspeakable. However, Symeon does provide his audience with the lasting impact even from this first of many experiences: "*The light envelops me* and appears to me like a star, and is incomprehensible to all. It is radiant like the sun, and *I perceive all creation encompassed by it*. It shows me all that it contains, and *enjoins me to respect my own limits*" (emphasis added). Symeon's revelatory experience—as best he can relate it—"envelops" him and gives him a sense of unity with all creation. Yet he still has a sense of his "own limits." And Symeon understands the purpose of such a grandiose vision: "To those who come near us we shall become 'light' and 'salt' *(cf. Mt. 5:13–14)* to their great benefit in Christ Jesus our Lord...."[60]

Another of his visions of light describes a lasting effect. While contemplating a sacred image (icon) of the Virgin Mary known as *Theotokos* ("God-bearer"), Symeon has yet another encounter with the Divine:

As I fell before [the icon], before I rose up, Thou Thyself didst appear to me within my poor heart, *as though thou hadst transformed it into light*; and then I knew that *I have Thee consciously within me*. From then onwards I loved Thee, not by recollection of Thee and that which surrounds Thee, nor from the memory of such things, but I in very truth believed that *I had Thee, substantial love, within me*. For Thou, O God, truly art love.[61]

From that point on, Symeon had a lasting notion of God's light, himself becoming "God-bearer." He never lost sight of that reality, and perhaps it was from that moment that he gained lasting assurance of the indwelling Trinity to which he was certain all had access. The experience continuously framed the outlook for himself and others.

Awareness of God's Indwelling

In "Hymn 50," Symeon asks the tantalizing question: "And how is it that one made god by grace and by adoption / will not be god in *awareness and knowledge and contemplation*, / he who has put on the Son of God?" He answers his rhetorical question with his take on Trinitarian theology: "I am entirely god by *sharing in God* in a *conscious awareness* / and by knowledge, not by essence / *but by participation*, as is absolutely necessary to believe to be orthodox" (emphasis added).[62] Symeon is *aware* of God within because he *participates* in the Trinity through the work of Christ. Recalling the unitive revelations of John's Gospel, as the Father is in the Son, and the Son is in the Father, Jesus prays that his disciples, too, will be joined to the Divine Unity (John 17:21, 23). Based on this lived truth, Symeon can say with confidence that, while the Father and Son are eternally united, the faithful too can participate through "adoption and grace."[63] The Byzantine monastic speaks with experiential authority when he preaches to his charges on the indwelling of God:

> When the soul by a good zeal has reached this state it is identified with God and becomes the *house and abode of the Divine Trinity. It sees its own Maker and God clearly*, and as it converses with Him day by day departs from the body and the world and from this air and ascends into the heaven of heavens (emphasis added).[64]

And while some objected to the "common person's" access to this type of awareness and participation, Symeon insisted—

based on his own reality—that such objections were not only in
error, but also encroached upon blaspheming the power of the
Spirit.[65]

As we move to close this section of the chapter, it is appropriate to rely on the beauty of Symeon's hymnody to express
truly his gift of indwelling awareness. He begins "Hymn 7" with
an open and longing heart:

> How do I adore You within myself and yet I perceive
>   You at a distance?
> How do I embrace You within me and I see You in the
>   heavens?
> You alone know it, You, the author of these things who
>   shine like
> the sun in my heart, my material heart, immaterially,
> you who made the light of Your glory shine on me, O
>   my God. . . .[66]

Symeon is confronted by the age-old conundrum of God:
How can the Ultimate Reality be immanently present, yet simultaneously transcendent? In the end, he does not attempt to solve
the riddle; he is content to be present in the reality as he experiences it.

CONCLUSION

Symeon's awareness of God within himself stood out to his contemporaries and to those who know of his legacy these many
centuries later. While common to the mystical experience of the
East, his use of light imagery to capture his indescribable encounters with the Transcendent nevertheless reveals a personal
spirituality that clings to God yet is also determined to share
that accessibility with others. What is exceptional about

Symeon's contemplative life is the primacy of contrition, expressed in prayers for purity, tears, and impassibility. Not seen as purely a preliminary step, constant compunction for Symeon was essential for any Christian to attain the conditions necessary to commune with God.[67] His visions of the Divine prompted one author, George Maloney, to rightly confer on him the lasting nickname "Mystic of Fire and Light," and his efforts for others to likewise perceive this truth affirm the church's designation of "the New Theologian."

Before concluding, let us consider Symeon's first theophany of light in his own words (in the third person of "George"):

> One day, as he stood and recited, "God, have mercy upon me, a sinner" *(Lk 18:13)*, uttering it with his mind rather than his mouth, suddenly a flood of divine radiance appeared from above and filled the room. As this happened the young man lost all awareness [of his surroundings] and forgot that he was in a house or that he was under a roof. He saw nothing but light all around him and did not know if was standing on the ground. He was not afraid of falling; he was not concerned with the word, nor did anything pertaining to men and corporeal beings enter into his mind. Instead, he was wholly in the presence of immaterial light and seemed to himself to have turned into light.[68]

Symeon's account raises questions for the postmodern thinker as to the "reality" of this experience, the descriptions lending themselves to a delusional or even pathological state of mind. Journeying toward the findings of contemporary neuropsychological research related to contemplative prayer and the brain provides some provocative answers.

4

The Contemplative Brain

One of the participants in the pastor's three-month study was an avid outdoorsman. He spent as much time as possible outside, whether going on hikes, building Habitat for Humanity homes, or enjoying the sights from the comfort of his back porch. For him, nothing was more rewarding than passing time in fresh air and the sights of creation. However, toward the end of the study period, the parishioner noticed something different about his time outdoors—images were more vivid, birdsong was more rhythmic, and the air was fresher. His awareness of his surroundings had intensified significantly. He was increasingly sensing the Divine Presence, and it was speaking to him through sights and experiences he had had hundreds of times before. But now they were different; his attention had shifted, and his interpretation of those experiences was being transformed too. His perception was changing.

We translate experience through interpretation. Ice is cold; music can be loud; on cloudless days, the sun is bright. "Cold," "loud," and "bright" are interpretations of sensory inputs (touch, sound, sight), interpretations that are fashioned by culture, stored in our memory, reinforced by time, and then revisited and recalled when seemingly appropriate. This parsing and filtration is the process of *perception*. But these ostensible realities may differ from person to person. For one, an eighty-five-pound, black Labrador retriever represents an irresistible thing to be stroked and doted on. For another, that same animal poses a menacing threat—as do all dogs—ever since that fateful childhood day of being attacked by a German shepherd that leapt the fence and exacted revenge upon *its* perceived antagonist. Perception is a function of experience.[1]

As we noted in chapter 1, perception does not simply have to do with *what* we see; it relates to *how* we see. In the example of the Labrador above, both people see an eighty-five-pound black dog. However, the first person perceives something to be loved; the second understands it as something to be feared. The respective *meanings* they assign to their sensory inputs stand in diametric opposition. Because all "realities" are ultimately the result of the cognitive process, we understand the brain as the primary actor in how we receive both the world *and* the transcendent. Any shift in worldview, then, must presumably be accompanied by a change in the brain's structure and/or operation to be sustained. Considering our thesis that contemplative prayer plays a role in shaping perception, the implication is clear that contemplation in some way facilitates such a physiological change.

In this chapter, we will examine the *neurological* effects of contemplative prayer, specifically the *processes* that are activated by these methods, and how the brain's *structures* can potentially be altered by intentional practice. Since there are *psychological* outcomes that attend these biological changes, we will also investigate contemplation's relationship to *optimal experience*, our *sense of self*, and our *external perspectives*.

CONTEMPLATION AND NEUROLOGICAL CHANGE

In the context of this work, neurological change presupposes a preliminary distinction between the *brain* and the *mind*. "Neurotheology" researcher and radiologist Andrew Newberg and his co-authors concisely define the *brain* as "a collection of physical structures that gather and process sensory, cognitive, and emotional data."[2] For some time, scientists have understood the brain in its basic functionality. The *left hemisphere* of the cerebrum is concerned with analytical processes like spoken language and mathematical computation, while the *right hemisphere* takes a holistic approach to sensory input, lending nuance and helping to shape meaning. Both sides work in conjunction with one another to paint a full, contextual picture. The two hemispheres are further subdivided into four lobes, each having a unique relationship with sensory processing. The *frontal lobe* is responsible for body movements, conscious decision-making, and executive functions. The *parietal lobe*, located about two-thirds of the way back, is concerned with the localization of touch and external sensations. The *temporal lobe*, on the side of the cerebrum, plays a major role in hearing, self-experience, and memory, and it also connects directly to the limbic system, the portion of the brain associated with intense emotions. The fourth and final subdivision is the *occipital lobe*, which resides in the back of the cerebrum and is concerned primarily with the regulation of vision. Meanwhile, the bases for the brain and its myriad functions are tens of billions of *neurons*, nerve cells that generate and communicate information, and are quite subject to reorganization.[3]

Abstracted from the physical brain is the concept of the *mind*. Newberg and his team define this as "the phenomenon of thoughts, memories, and emotions that arise from the perceptual processes of the brain."[4] In other words, the mind is how the brain essentially "sees" itself. It is a product of all the various neurobiological processes, a "self-perception" that is naturally susceptible to the corresponding structural changes in the underlying neural infrastructure. However, somewhat counterintuitively, modern research has demonstrated that thoughts —mental activity that results from neural processes—can conversely influence how brain circuitry is physically wired. We will use the beacon of neurophysiology to help pierce the dense fog of this transformational conundrum.

Building Perceptions

Since perception is the interpretation of sensory input, we begin with a glimpse of the regions of the brain that are primarily responsible for interpretative processing. These locations in the temporal, parietal, and occipital lobes are known as *association areas* because they are the geographical centers where information from all over the brain is aggregated and analyzed. For example, raw image data from the eyes and optic nerves is routed to the occipital lobe, and then, after other data is amassed, that picture is passed to the *visual association area*. Once there, memory and emotion are "associated" with the image to give it full meaning; with these additional inputs—conceptions, labels, context—the image is converted to a full-blown perception. There are four known association areas: *visual, orientation, attention,* and *verbal conceptual.*[5] Two of these—orientation and attention—play critical roles during contemplative prayer. We explore their functions below.

Three smaller yet equally significant parts of the brain also help shape our perception. The *thalamus*, located in the center of the brain between the two hemispheres, serves as a "gateway" of sorts for sensory information to pass into proper association areas. The thalamus has a particularly important role with regard to memory and emotional traffic. Meanwhile, the *hypothalamus*, resting just below the thalamus, exerts control over the autonomic nervous system and plays a central role during intense contemplative engagement.[6] Essential to memory storage is the *hippocampus*. This seahorse-shaped structure inside the temporal lobe plays "traffic cop" for the movement of information around the brain and translates new information to long-term memory.[7] Each of these three areas is key to contemplative experience and the formation of perceptions.

Now, the *autonomic nervous system* (ANS) is an extension of the brain that plays a foundational role in our makeup. It functions "involuntarily" or without conscious thought to control vital functions like heartbeat and the breathing and is regulated by the hypothalamus. Its two parts, the *sympathetic nervous system* (SNS) and the *parasympathetic nervous system* (PNS), complement each other when engaged by external stimuli. The former is active when organs or processes need a burst of energy (e.g., in the so-called fight or flight scenario); the latter serves to return things to homeostasis.[8]

Specific labels are assigned to the "intense engagement" of these systems. In the case of the SNS, *hyperarousal* is marked by high attentiveness; the person is completely immersed in an activity, especially one of potential risk to the participant. At the other end of the spectrum, *hyperquiescence* refers to the experience of extreme serenity, all external stimuli seemingly blocked out by inner calm. When one of these conditions exists, its counterpart is typically inactive. There are situations, however, when both the SNS and the PNS may be at work simultaneously, a state known as *spillover*. *Hyperarousal/quiescence* is a condition of ecstatic experience that peaks with an overarching sense of tranquility or euphoria. *Hyperquiescence/arousal* describes a deep, blissful experience that leads to extreme awe or profundity, sometimes described as a sense of "absorption."[9] In what follows, we explore how these ANS conditions, their regulators, and the brain's various association areas contribute to the contemplative experience.

Neural Processes of Contemplation

Contemplation can be divided into two domains: one that makes use of attention or focus, and another the aim of which is to clear the mind of thoughts and distractions, keeping it virtually "open." Christian practices that use icons or other visual foci, repetitive prayers, or self-reflection techniques fall into the first category.[10] Variations on the so-called Centering Prayer and those concerned with mindfulness and/or breath-awareness are examples of the latter type. Some label the focused prayers "active" in their nature; the others they term "passive."[11] The neural processes involved in each type are somewhat different, yet their ultimate influence on perception is similar. Newberg's modeling sheds light on how all the processes function in concert.

On the active side of prayer, the intent is focus. Since "willful" activities are thought to be initiated by the right attention area of the brain, this location is where our Rube Goldberg-like journey begins. From there, the thalamus serves as a "messaging gatekeeper," alerting the hippocampus to intensify the neural flow to the right orientation area (the part concerned with spatial context) and the appropriate sensory-related association area (e.g., the visual center in the case of iconic focus). After sustained contemplative concentration, the right attention area is flooded with neural activity, filtering out all sensory input except the object or idea on which it is centered. This process continuously loops, reinforcing itself like a hurricane gaining energy from the warm waters below. At some point, the effect is overwhelming to the hypothalamus, and it triggers the SNS, leading to the state of hyperarousal.

If the intensity of the event continues to increase, the situation we know as "spillover" can occur. At that point, the hypothalamus activates the PNS to counteract the excitement and help restore equilibrium. However, because the neural flow is reverberating throughout the brain, both the SNS and the PNS continue to function simultaneously; in this elevated state, the contemplative has now entered the realm of hyperarousal/quiescence. With the SNS and PNS collaborating, neural flow to the attention area—the seat of focus—is at its absolute peak. Meanwhile, since the hippocampus is redirecting all neural resources toward the attention center, the left orientation area (the place that defines the "geographic" sense of self) lacks input. This invariably leads to a condition called *deafferation*—a total loss of the boundaries of self. In parallel, the right orientation area is bombarded with signals from the right attention area, which now only knows one thing—the target of concentration. Since the bounded self has melted away, the only contextual reference that remains is that target. The result is that the contemplative and the item merge into one.[12] Our mystic's experience from the previous chapter is an example of this phenomenon.

Symeon the New Theologian's "Discourse 22" illustrates a possible outcome of active contemplation. The following excerpt, told in third person, reveals the mystic's experience, at least as he was able to describe it after the fact:

One day, as he stood and recited, [A] "God, have mercy upon me, a sinner" *(Lk 18:13)*, uttering it with his mind rather than his mouth, suddenly [B] a flood of divine radiance appeared from the above and filled all the room. As this happened the young man [C] lost all awareness [of his surroundings] and forgot that he was in a house or that he was under a roof. He saw nothing but light all around him and did not know if he was standing on the ground. He was not afraid of falling; [D] he was not concerned with the word, nor did anything pertaining to men and corporeal beings enter his mind. Instead, he was wholly in the presence of immaterial light and [E] seemed to himself to have turned into the light.[13]

As we analyze this text, we see several indications of a classic hyperarousal/quiescence state. First, we can classify the prayer as "active" because Symeon is mentally repeating the phrase, "God, have mercy upon me, a sinner," a version of the Jesus Prayer (A).[14] Second, we assume his visual focus rests on the singular source of light in the room, his burning lamp, as that practice was common for Symeon (B).[15] Next, we understand that Symeon is experiencing deafferation, as he has lost his bearings to the point where he does not know whether or not he is standing (C). Because his neural flow is purely in attention mode, other sensory association areas like the verbal concept center are void of input, such that "he was not concerned with the word," and nothing else occupied his mind (D). Finally, we see the ultimate end of deafferation and complete focus in the visual center, as Symeon reports that he himself has become the light that he "sees" (E).

Admittedly, Symeon's report of this account is nothing short of mysterious. The subjectivity of his story cannot be "scientifically" validated, nor can his emotional state of mind be evaluated some ten centuries later. However, given his descriptions of an otherwise ineffable occurrence, they uniquely follow the processes we have described for "active" prayer.

For *passive* forms of prayer, the processes tend to parallel their active counterparts, but with notable differences. The idea of clearing the mind of distractions is again initiated by the right attention area. The thalamus is the next actor, this time requesting the hippocampus to *dampen* all neural flow except that necessary to preclude thoughts in the attention areas. The cycling of this attention focus essentially deprives the rest of the system of all sensory input. The hypothalamus is bombarded with messaging, eventually igniting the PNS to go into an overdrive of calming activity—hyperquiescence. Continued intensity results once again in spillover, and so this time the hypothalamus signals the SNS to balance things out. The neural traffic is now very high in both nervous systems, and the state of hyperquiescence/arousal arrives as anticipated. However, something unique happens at this juncture. In the active approach, only the left orientation center is deprived of neural input, such that the boundaries of self are diminished. In this passive case, *both* orientation areas are starved of input (along with the visual and verbal conceptual centers), so not only has the sense of *self* been dissolved, but there is also an absence of spatial *context*. Time, space, and identity have disappeared, leaving the vastness of the "void" as the sole relational reference.[16] The contemplative has perceptually merged with infinity.

Meanwhile, the experience is ineffable post-prayer because the contemplative presumably has nothing to work with to describe what occurred. Another excerpt from Symeon's writings on contemplation validates this assertion:

> The mobile mind becomes motionless and unthinking—without thoughts—when it is entirely encompassed by the Divine cloud and light, at the same time remaining in conscious contemplation and apprehension, feeding on the blessings which surround it. The depths of the Holy Spirit are beyond understanding or explanation. [A] The mind enters therein after relinquishing everything visible and mental, and moves and turns motionlessly among these incomprehensible things, living a life more than life, being a light while yet in the light, though

no light when in itself. [B] Then it sees not itself but Him
Who is above it and, being inwardly transformed by the
glory surrounding it, loses all knowledge of itself.[17]

Reviewing his experience, we again find common ground
with the later stages of passive contemplation. We see the evidence of the deactivation of the visual and verbal conceptual association centers through Symeon's "relinquishing [of]
everything visible and mental," all things moving toward the
"incomprehensible" (A). And he perfectly describes the outcomes of total deafferation, noting that the mind "sees not itself
but Him Who is above," ultimately losing "all knowledge of itself" (B). Couching this physiological end stage in spiritual language, "the degree of oneness with both God and the real world
outside himself gives the mystic the simplified consciousness of
becoming the whole of reality."[18] Trials with modern contemplatives as subjects have validated these independent claims.

In 1999, Newberg and his team of researchers conducted
one of the first studies of its time: they convinced three Franciscan nuns to undergo imaging tests during their contemplative
"centering prayer" sessions.[19] Using a contemporary form of
neuroimaging technology, the scientists measured blood flow
throughout the brain as the nuns prayed. Their findings of flow
patterns through the frontal and parietal lobes and the thalamus
seemingly support the processes described above in relation to
the various association areas. In his book *How God Changes
Your Brain*, Newberg summarizes this transcendental formula:
"Frontal lobe activity increases, limbic activity decreases, and
the combination generates a peaceful and serene state of consciousness."[20] Later research corroborates these findings.

Inspired by the Newberg undertaking, other neuroscientists
later conducted similar experiments with a group of fifteen
Carmelite nuns.[21] Using current imaging tools, the team exam-

ined the contemplatives as they *recalled and relived* an intense "mystical" event. While the nuns were not actively praying during the imaging, the results nevertheless echoed Newberg's work. Most prominent in these researchers' observations were the activations of those areas associated with feelings of "joy and unconditional love," and the modifications to the orientation centers that would leave the "impression that something greater than the subjects had seemed to absorb them." All of these studies provide evidence that there are in fact neural correlates to contemplation and that there is a firm association between the praying mind and the underlying brain.

We should pause to note that analyzing contemplatives' prayer life from a neurophysiological perspective does not diminish their notion of mystical experience, whether they be medieval ascetics or a contemporary group of religious. We cannot be empirically certain of what happens to those who pray during these moments of divine encounter. We can, however, be confident that when the Spirit speaks, we have a finite means of receiving that message, and that perception begins with the faculties with which we are created—namely our neurophysiological systems. Likewise, we know that with such repeated encounters, structural changes do occur. Just as athletes condition their bodies to the point of "muscle memory," so the brain reshapes itself through repeated contemplative stimuli.

Prayer Conditioning

"The brain is simply an organ that repeats what it knows."[22] This statement originates with a therapist who assists her patients in recovering from traumatic brain injuries, and she is a firm believer in the power of the brain to reorganize itself structurally with the intent of reinforcing that repetition. This process is termed *neuroplasticity*, the "ability of neurons to forge new connections, to blaze new paths...even to assume new roles."[23] In the early stages of this science, researchers were attentive to sensory inputs as the source of these changes, first the amount of sensory data, then later the quality of that input. But as the science has matured, studies have shown that not only *external* stimuli can effect change, but so too can *internal* processes, that is, *thoughts*.[24]

Prayer always begins as a mental activity. As we have noted, contemplation is especially a cerebral exercise, with focusing and mindfulness techniques consuming significant mental energy. Since these practices are repetitive in nature and continuously "exercise" the same parts of the brain during contemplative experience, we presume that those impacted neural networks are likely to strengthen or reorganize over time. Additionally, given these presumed changes, a "new normal" should arise. Data from numerous studies buttress these ideas.

For example, Newberg and his team found that the neurological changes they observed in their subjects "were significant and very different from how the human brain normally functions." They attribute these changes to the duration of prayer, both temporally and longitudinally. While intermittent practice may not result in much variation, "forty minutes of daily practice, over a period of years, will bring permanent changes to the brain."[25] Engaging the various structures of the brain through prayer gradually alters their makeup.

More recent studies on contemplation and the brain focus on its default mode network (DMN). This DMN consists of regions within the frontal and parietal lobes, as well as the association areas near the back of the brain, that are most active when we are not engaged in intentional thought. The DMN is involved in several mental functions, but the most notable for our purposes are the acts of "mind wandering," introspection, and the overall assessment of "self."[26] Excessive mind wandering indicates a tendency to be frequently off-task, while incessant self-examination usually results in a negative assessment or self-image.[27] The common findings of the researchers is that those who engage in contemplative practices show significant changes in their brain anatomy as it relates to internal attention, emotional stability, and sensory reception. Furthermore, in keeping with our assumptions based on the characteristics of neuroplasticity, prolonged contemplation seems to create a "new normal," one in which the resting state of the DMN is far more "present-centered," even when not engaged in active contemplation.[28] All these indicators signify that contemplatives tend to be on-task, are less susceptible to criticism, and have a controlled sense of self-awareness—the contemplative brain rewires itself to a dispassionate state. Some researchers have picked up on these observations and promote contemplation as a means of change. Creativity specialist Shelley Carson provides two valuable examples.

Carson identifies seven "brainsets" or neural functions that apply to the creative process, and she promotes several means of activating them in her book, *Your Creative Brain*. Two of these have interesting applications to our conversation. First, the *absorb* brainset represents the brain in its receptive mode, "open to information generated in the external environment (the world) as well as from the internal environment (the mind)."[29] Here, the brain's filtering mechanisms are relaxed, and information is free to pass from the association centers into conscious awareness. This is akin to the contemplative's goal of detachment in that judgments are put to the side and thoughts are free to come and go without over-analysis. It is a critical condition that enables novel observations and opens the gateways to relevant connections.[30]

Carson recommends accessing this state via a passive discipline termed "openness meditation" (OM). OM includes an abiding consciousness of the breath. There is an awareness of thoughts, but the contemplative makes no effort to evaluate or attach to them. The sole intent is the rhythmic breath in a sense of "being."[31] Christian contemplatives recognize this practice as a variation on the Centering Prayer, with occasional attention to the breath substituted for Centering's mental "prayer word."

A second neural function is the *envision* brainset. This activation state facilitates imagination, a gift that allows us to see things beyond the boundaries of superficiality. Pragmatically, the envision brainset also "provides the neural basis" for how we construct a "coherent worldview and a sense of identity."[32] Envision is achieved through the practice of mental imagery. In this mode, the association areas of the brain typically involved with processing outside stimuli are engaged, yet their action is generated from "quasi perceptual" means, namely visualization. When we visualize, we deactivate the executive functions of the prefrontal cortex, but we activate the neurons that are responsible for sensory detection and interpretation, thereby training those parts of the brain and strengthening their ability to "see" (or hear, smell, feel, or taste) on demand.[33]

One of the exercises that Carson promotes to enhance the ability to generate "multi-modal" mental imagery is called "mental holiday." The practitioner imagines a space of familiar relaxation (like a beach or other locale), then takes a virtual tour of that space. Carson invites the "dreamer" to engage all the senses on the trip, including sights, sounds, sensations, and smells. Continuous practice results in "vivid" imagery, and simultaneously reduces verbal thought.[34] For the contemplative, these steps relate directly to those of "imaginative prayer" sourced from Ignatius of Loyola's *Spiritual Exercises*. In the "Fifth Contemplation" of the second week, the text directs the one who prays to bring "the five senses" to bear during the contemplation of Jesus's life in the Gospels. The practice prescribes complete sensual engagement in the stories, with visualization being key to entering the sacred mystery of scripture. By imagining these scenes and experiencing them mentally, the contemplative is immersed in the worldview of Christ, identifying with him (or others) in the passages.[35]

Spiritual disciplines are "essential to cognitive transformation," itself the root of behavioral change.[36] We have seen so far that contemplation facilitates not only activation of the areas of the brain that relate to building positive perceptions, but that contemplatives actively reorganize their neural circuitry in a way that reinforces those cognitive processes for future functioning. And once reorganized, the resulting perceptions that arise from this spiritual practice take on a semi-permanence, subject only to future changes that may emerge. This permanence, in turn, is manifested via observable mental changes.

CONTEMPLATION AND PSYCHOLOGICAL PHENOMENA

As discussed, the mind's activity—thoughts—can influence the neural reorganization of the brain. More intuitively, we also understand that changes to the underlying structure of the brain manifest themselves in our thoughts, and thereby our behaviors. It's a symbiotic "chicken or egg" conundrum that somewhat defies examination. Nevertheless, the relationship is real, and so there is a logical implication that contemplation can affect our mentation, either directly or indirectly. These influences show up in many ways related to perception, but the results are particularly pronounced as they relate to *presence*, *self-perception*, and the *adoption of a new worldview*.

A Sense of Presence
In our earlier discussion of the brain's default mode, we recognized from research on mindfulness that contemplatives tend toward a greater sense of *presence* in their daily disposition. This state of being "in the moment" is characterized by a mind

that disregards distractions and remains singularly focused yet is simultaneously open to possibility. This state of mind is known as "flow." Flow is the sense of "consciousness [being] harmoniously ordered," where the sage-like pursuit of a given task is completely unitary and wholly enjoyable.[37] There are nine "conditions" for flow to be present, and while most are uniquely relevant to presence, we briefly highlight five for their direct correlation to contemplation. First, action and awareness are seemingly combined. This "one-pointedness of mind" is facilitated by mindfulness contemplation that allows the practitioner to hone his or her attention. Second, distractions are excluded from consciousness. As already noted, the contemplative builds the ability to block out the "noise" of external and internal disturbances, marking them as irrelevant to the moment. Third, there is no concern regarding "failure." Success and failure are judgmental land mines that the contemplative mind is wired to avoid. Fourth, the sense of self-consciousness is absent. The ability to withhold judgment begins with the self; caring about external opinions is subdued through the contemplative's developed *apatheia*. Finally, the person in a state of flow loses the sense of chronological time. Symptomatic of deafferation, the contemplative's notion of spatial time dissolves, leaving only a raw sense of the now.[38] The mind of presence and its perceptibility is one that "exhibits an open and translucent quality through which reality is experienced in a clear and less conditioned way," possibly "on the path to the nondual and unconditioned consciousness described in many traditions." Some researchers grasp the potential of developing this mind, and they understand the transformational possibilities of its attainment. And what do they suggest as the "most effective way" of moving toward this mind? The practice of "some form of regular meditation or contemplation."[39] Contemplative prayer is essential for the proper development of presence.

Contemplation and Self-Perception

Contemplation is also a staple in developing a clear perspective of the self. Whatever appears in our minds is a result of attention, and that attentional impetus is known in some circles as "psychic energy." Our investment of this energy is directly correlated to our creation of "self."[40] If we give attention to the negative aspects of our lives, the mind becomes trained to see through the filter of that negativity. However, if we apply psychic energy in ways that promote more positive processes—presence, detachment, and even attention—the self becomes constructively reinforcing. This form of consciousness experiences the "mundane" as special, and it merges the temporal with the sacred.[41] "Self," then, takes on new meaning, both differentiated in its enhanced ability to "be," yet simultaneously integrated into the greater whole as one who understands how he or she is woven into the fabric of society and creation. This increased complexity relates to psychological growth.

As our sense of self within reality expands, so too does our identity with the community. "Wholeness brings clarity" and causes us to expand outward from ourselves toward the "object" of our perception.[42] For the contemplative, this "object" lies wholly outside the self-seeking intentions of self-gratification or personal gain. The late psychologist Abraham Maslow of the "hierarchy of needs" fame called this experience "ego-transcending, self-forgetful, egoless, [and] unselfish."[43] In this positive movement, the mind assembles its inputs to reinforce its own ideas of wholeness and purpose, consistent in its thoughts and equally constant in the resulting behaviors. As in a continuous state of flow, the contemplative seeks the overall goals of internal and external integrity with a singular mind, with distractions and perceptions that oppose this end gaining no foothold in the consciousness. What emerges is a consciousness that, in the spiritual language of Cynthia Bourgeault, attempts to "eradicate the ground of sin," because it "completely expose[s] that small-self 'I' who always has some stake in the matter, some vested self-interest."[44] And, once again, psychologists point to the spiritually based practices of contemplation as the mechanism of choice to reframe this self-perception.

Recalling the concept of "psychic energy," mastering that energy—enabling ourselves to direct our attention toward self-growth—requires a means of harnessing it for proper use. Spiritual techniques of contemplation are most valuable toward this end, and the rigors of practices like the *Spiritual Exercises* are favorable to some psychologists.[45] Contemplation metaphorically polishes the mind for a clearer sense of self to shine forth, exhibiting "a slow but continuously abrasive effect on mental agitations, gradually leading to a cleansing of the mental grit that impedes the smooth flow of consciousness."[46]

The mind precedes the self in that it contains all the raw materials from which the self can construct its reality.[47] In other words, as the mind goes, so goes the sense of self. By influencing the raw materials themselves, contemplative activity hones the powers of attention; simultaneously, this reframes self-perception through a conscious outward movement from the ego-centric "I" to the unified "we." The self that emerges as a result has a new sense of priority and purpose, untainted by stimuli that would distract from its cause. And as the perception of self expands, so too does its understanding of the world.

Contemplation and a Transformed View of the World
Our final psychological phenomenon is the contemplative's *adoption of a new worldview*. When the mind interprets its inputs in an entirely new way, perceptions shift. Experiences have new and/or evolved meanings, and our responses adapt accordingly— we begin to "see" differently. Creativity is related to this changed perception, and our worldview is reflected in its expression.

Episcopal priest and modern mystic Matthew Fox boldly proclaims that *"our true nature is our creativity."*[48] We are made to ascend beyond the concrete to the farthest reaches of possibility, to attend to our fullest potential. To envision this future requires broad perception, a seeing that begins with imagination. For Fox, the goal of imagination is "liberation itself," the key to unlocking the bounded world of an enclosed existence.[49] As research demonstrates, contemplative approaches to prayer have a direct correlation with generating divergent or "out-of-the-box" ideas.

Ideation as a function of creativity is a key indicator of imaginative output. Standard divergent thought tests administered to experienced active and passive contemplatives reveal that the total number of responses (*fluency*) and the number of different categories for those responses (*flexibility*) are statistically higher than the norm.[50] Passive contemplation's activation of our "open-mindedness" may be at the root of this method's results, while the tendency for active meditation to "uplift" our mood is the driver for that style's efficacy.[51] Taken together, the results of these studies reinforce the claim that contemplative prayer enhances our ability to be imaginatively creative, a key component of seeing the world in a novel way. Other aspects of creativity also signal a changed outlook.

Completing the statement, "When I'm creative I am...," a psychologist compiled a list of twelve possible psychological "benefits" of living a creative life.[52] Each of these aspects has an obvious connection to the contemplative outcome of changed perception. Persons living creatively are: (1) dynamic—seeing change and understanding that they are part of an evolving system; (2) conscious—actively aware of and attentive to internal and external stimuli; (3) healthy—living a life in physical and psychological (and spiritual) balance; (4) non-defensive—limiting forces that could lead to inner negativity; (5) open—operating within a high state of detachment, therefore welcoming thoughts and experiences without judgment; (6) integrating—functioning across multiple domains of consciousness and perspective, moving from complexity to simplicity; (7) observing—constantly in dialogue with the environment, actively or passively; (8) caring—living a life of love and compassion, with awareness of a larger unity; (9) collaborative—acting as co-creators with others; (10) androgynous—bridging false dichotomies despite social stereotypes; (11) developing—constantly emerging and evolving; and (12) brave—welcoming the unknown in trust of life's processes.[53] All these traits are transformative in nature, and as we have seen in previous paragraphs, each can be directly linked to contemplation. In realizing these benefits, contemplatives "might even come to see self and life in whole new way."[54]

CONCLUSION

"Consciousness is more than perceiving and knowing; it is *knowing* that you know."[55] This enigmatic statement captures the paradoxical relationship between the brain and the mind. One—the brain—obviously provides the core "stuff" through which the other—the mind—finds fulfillment. Nevertheless, we have seen that the latter can influence the neural circuitry of the former through pure "will." Meanwhile, perception sits as a product of both simply organic reception of inputs and the mental interpretation of those same stimuli. And since contemplative prayer is an effective agent of change for both the physiological and psychological domains, it plays a unique role in its ability to change human experience.

While not receiving an overwhelmingly welcome response in the scientific community, associating the spiritual disciplines with the neuropsychological world has steadily gained traction since the 1990s. The body of research specifically considering contemplative practices continues to grow. As a vocal champion of this cause, Newberg makes a provocative statement:

> Mystical reality holds, and neurology does not contradict it, that beneath the mind's perception of thoughts, memories, emotions, and objects, beneath the subjective awareness we think of as the self, there is a deeper self, a state of pure awareness that sees beyond the limits of subject and object, and rests in a universe where all things are one.[56]

Traditional scientific inquiry tends to shy away from exploring such ostensibly non-empirical ideas. However, in his most recent work, *Neurotheology*, Newberg blends, as the title suggests, the topics of neurology, psychology, and theology in ways that respectfully yet critically approach all three disciplines.[57] His conclusions and the conclusions of others certainly seem to overlap with those of many contemporary Christian theologians who examine the faith with postmodern eyes and hearts. In the next chapter, based on their insights and revolutionary interpretations of the Gospel message, we attempt to synthesize the biblical, historical, and neuropsychological wisdom gained thus far.

5

The Mind of Christ

One of the participants in the ninety-day study struggled with the process early on. The pastor had asked the group to read Psalm 23 as the second of four steps of their daily regimen, and it seemed that the repetition of the psalm somehow set off deep-seated resentments for this pray-er. Those feelings surfaced with a good amount of intensity and regularity, but nevertheless, he persevered.

Several weeks into the practice, the participant experienced a breakthrough. He started noticing the angry emotions when they first began to rise, as they were wont to do. Engaging them systematically, he questioned the rationality of his previous responses, rooting out the weeds of entanglement that were littering his experience of the contemplation and himself. Gradually, the tensions eased, until, near the end of the three months, the psalm's antagonistic quality had dissolved. He had overcome his emotions, and the resulting clarity revealed an underlying joy that proved refreshingly welcome.

In John's Gospel, Thomas responds to a presumed literal statement from Jesus with an equally one-dimensional question, "How can we know the way?" Jesus responds, however, with the multifaceted and cosmic truth: "I am the way, and the truth, and the life" (14:5–6). The word translated as "way" (*hodos*) in this verse, as Thomas presumes, denotes a path or road by which a traveler may reach a destination. However, Jesus's figurative usage here doesn't presume a destination, but a *destiny*— life with God. Jesus pronounces that the life he embodies—his "way"—is nothing less than "an expression of the faithful person's unity with God."[1] Two medieval saints understood this relationship to God through Christ.

Although not literally a Franciscan, Clare of Assisi was a protégé of Francis himself. She was a church innovator in her own right. Bonaventure, a thirteenth-century Franciscan monk, was eventually named a Doctor of the Church for his theological brilliance. Bonaventure knew Christ as the true revelation of the Father, and he posited that we tend toward that ideal as creatures formed in God's likeness. Therefore, the human person is an image of *the* Image of God—Jesus the Christ. Clare, meanwhile, also knew humanity as being created *ad imaginem*, or "to the image," of Christ. For her, "image" meant both "a structure and a goal," simultaneously something to emulate *and* something to become. Clare is known for her metaphor of the crucified Christ as a mirror, reflecting the image of "what we are to be in our lives."[2] Combining these similar thoughts, we conclude that God through Christ not only reveals how we are to be *human* ("the truth"), but also patterns how that life is lived eternally *in God* ("the life"). Both begin with repentance.

At the outset of his public ministry, Jesus proclaims, "Repent, for the kingdom of heaven has come near" (Matt 4:17; cf. Mark 1:5; Luke 13:3–5). Here, "repent" (*metanoeite*) is a verb that literally means "to change one's mind" or "think differently after."[3] Jesus's declaration implies no bit of casual thinking, but a complete rearrangement of perception and outlook, a process with life-changing outcomes. This new outlook involves death to the old ways and the experience of new life ahead (cf. Eph 4:22–24). Jesus models this self-sacrifice via the passion of the cross and then provides a portal through which we glimpse life on the other side.

In this chapter, we draw upon the prior discussions of this work to form a theological synthesis. We also examine how the practice of contemplative prayer can lead to a transformation modeled by Christ. It begins with *death*—death to the *world's alternatives*, and ultimately to the "*self*" we once knew. Through this agonizing process—and the work of the Spirit— we potentially make a breakthrough; on the other side, we "awaken" to a new world, a world in which our perceptions have changed. We begin to see life as Christ sees, with eyes of *compassion* that result from *unified perception*, as we have in a sense been *resurrected*. Understanding this renewing action of death and resurrection through contemplation, we then consider Jesus's work of *atonement* through this newly ground lens.

THE CROSS: DYING TO THE WORLD AND TO "SELF"

In the three Synoptic Gospels, Jesus remains silent to the powers of the world: he is questioned; he is beaten; he is hauled away and subjected to a death reserved for the most despicable members of society. Yet, despite these seemingly dire consequences, his response to the "authorities" is restricted to three words: "You say so" (Matt 27:11; cf. Mark 15:2; Luke 23:3). John's account is the only place we see any sustained exchange between Christ and the Roman establishment, and these, too, are telling. In the face of Pilate's questioning, Jesus affirms twice that his "kingdom is not from this world" (John 18:36). And as Pilate argues his own legitimacy, Jesus trumps his claims: "You would have no power over me unless it had been given you from above" (John 19:11). It is clear from these gospel accounts that the faithful are not to engage the so-called world—social constructs of purely human origin—without proper perspective. Emulating Christ on the cross, the same applies to our notion of "self."

In his meditations on the "seven last words of Christ," theologian Stanley Hauerwas reveals how Jesus's action on the cross represents a complete and total death to self. He redirects the potentially narcissistic interpretation of this divine work away from ourselves and refocuses it on the primary actor in this cosmic drama—God. Hauerwas's take on three of these meditations are particularly useful to our conversation. In the fourth "word," Jesus's cry of dereliction (cf. Matt 27:46) is not some strange separation of the Godhead, but an "outworking of the mystery called Trinity." It is the image of a God who demonstrates an abandonment of self through perfect love.[4] In the sixth meditation, "It is finished" (John 19:30), he presses past the obvious of Jesus's death to a larger, universal purpose—the consummation of creation. It is a victorious exclamation, one that signifies the end of "our vain attempts to be our own creators," and one that evokes peace because "God has given us a way to live without answers."[5] Lastly, the seventh passage or "word" presumes a silent, terrorizing moment of the unknown. Jesus commends his spirit to the Father and quite literally dies (Luke 23:46), thereby embodying a God who endures the "dark night of death."[6] In short, the crucifixion encapsulates the idea of *kenosis*—an emptying, a claiming of true identity and purpose, and an inevitable passage through the shadows of death.

Jesus set the condition of discipleship as the need for self-denial through the cross (cf. Matt 16:24). As we have noted, that journey implies a transition, a death to our view of the world and to our "selves." Let us now consider the role of contemplative prayer in this transition.

Death to the World: Apatheia

The world provides a plethora of distractions. Ad agencies bombard us with scientifically crafted messaging that plays to our wants. Politicians prey upon our basest emotions, broadcasting divisive slogans and promoting tactics that deepen our fears and anxieties. Electronic media shrink the global domain, allowing for immediate gratification and distorting the notion of "friend."[7] As already noted, the mind through the organic functioning of the brain is how we receive these inputs, and our perceptions are shaped accordingly. Elia Delio captures the problem and tone of our postmodern world:

> The problems of our age—war, conflict, racial and religious injustice, economic greed, power, corruption, control and manipulation, lying and deceit—are human problems. *We have literally lost our minds.* We have untethered the human mind from any higher levels of consciousness, allowing our mind to wander aimlessly amid fields of uncensored information, burdening the mind with emotional and psychological baggage, copious amounts of junk information, and dousing the mind with alcohol and drugs periodically. We have the equivalent of a fast-food problem with regard to the mind or, I would say, "junk-food minds" (emphasis added).[8]

As these inputs of "junk-food" increasingly compete for our attention, the message of the gospel becomes diluted and, in some cases, pushed aside altogether. When this occurs, we develop into what the late mystic Thomas Merton termed "exterior" people. The "exterior" person "tends to look at things from the economic or technical or hedonistic viewpoint which, in spite of all its pragmatic advantages, certainly removes the seer from direct contact with the reality which he [or she] sees."[9] This mind develops over time, with emotions, past experiences, and new (misleading?) data helping shape misperception. What is lacking is a means to filter these inputs that serve as causal agents.

Apatheia has been defined in a wide range of ways. Some mean it to be synonymous with "dispassionate," the person free from overwhelming or lopsided emotions and functioning like a sage in his or her daily choices and actions. Others take it even further, equating *apatheia* with the reactionless state of "impassibility." Persons in this condition are completely immovable, unfazed by life as it happens around them.[10] Whatever the connotation, *apatheia*, at its core, represents a condition in which we are no longer easily distracted by what the world tosses our way. As for Christ, God takes center stage, and the awareness of that presence stills all external stimuli.

Symeon the New Theologian, our mystic from chapter 3, expresses this death to the world in compelling tenth-century language. He understood that the contemplative's posture toward the world's values was one of distance. He did not have contempt for material things or social status per se, but he feared that people had elevated the interpretation of these objects and institutions to idolatrous heights. He attempts to illustrate just such confusion:

Those who with the help of the Holy Spirit have been vouchsafed union with God and have tasted of His ineffable blessings, no longer delight in empty—I would even say dishonorable and worthless—glory had from men. Neither do they wish for money, costly garments, or precious stones, as the foolish call them: they do not love to be attached or to cleave with [their] hearts to transitory and inconstant riches, passing from one man to another; they do not love to be known to kings and potentates who are not true princes, lords and rulers, since they are possessed and ruled by many passions. Such men do not regard them as high and mighty and do not think that they bestow any special glory on their familiars. Neither do they aspire to be close to any other famous or renowned men of the world, since no man cares to exchange riches for poverty or to become dishonoured, bereft of glory, despicable and lowest of all, instead of being a great and powerful lord covered in glory.[11]

Symeon considered the ideals of the world to be misplaced. Just as Christ metaphorically located those whose priorities were off among the "dead" (Matt 8:22; Luke 9:60), so too did Symeon draw a stark line for the perceptions of the faithful: "For the saints, the world and people in it are dead."[12]

The mindfulness of Christ through contemplation was what Symeon prescribed to his monastic charges to achieve this detachment:

Likewise a monk who, having truly abandoned the world and all worldly things, has come to Christ and, incited by right emotional perception . . . has risen to the heights of spiritual contemplation, contemplates God without prelest [spiritual delusion] and sees clearly the transformation effected in him. For he is constantly aware of the grace of the Holy Spirit illumining him, which is called both a garment and royal purple. For believers, this garment is Jesus Christ Himself, since those who believe in Him are clothed in Him.[13]

Through experience, Symeon understood that constant meditation on God in Christ changes the disposition of the heart and mind. Attention to this reality, rather than the concerns of the "world," attunes awareness in a singular fashion. This practice is akin to mindfulness, and, as we discovered in the previous chapter, it weans the mind off external stimuli and allows deeper focus on the task at hand.

In 2017, *Time* magazine published a special summer edition featuring various entries that speak to presence and its impact on our daily lives.[14] One such article notes the effects of contemplation on detachment. Quoting another researcher, the author notes that consistent, intentional practice of mindfulness can help improve our ability "to accept things without strongly attaching to them." Additionally, the value of this type of *apatheia* is that, while the emotions that arise from the world's inputs may still come, our response to these passions is short-lived: "There's no lingering, no stickiness."[15] The old feelings that consume our lives are compartmentalized, cached in their rightful place of non-influential noise. Contemplation nullifies their effects, thereby allowing us to form different perceptions that align with the faith. Contemplative prayer is a conscious act of dying to the world.

Jesus refused to hear the noise of society. It challenged him with the enticing definitions of life, power, and authority (Luke 4:1–13; cf. Matt 4:1–11), but understanding the true source of all these, he was dead to that false reality of the "world." On the cross, he died to self too.

Death to the Self: Kenosis

With life on the cross, death is inevitable. It is the ultimate end to what has come before, and the gate through which we pass into the mystery of what lies ahead. It marks a transition from one reality to another, and for Jesus there was no exception. Yet there was an aspect of his act that was peculiar: his assumption of the cross was *voluntary*, a "death freely accepted." He relinquished his claim to divinity and offered up his embodied humanity as a means of cosmic reconciliation, simultaneously obliterating logical notions of messiahship and the mortal tendency for self-preservation. He died with intent through an act of *kenosis*. Hauerwas's model helps us to understand Christ's archetypical release as relived through contemplation.

Kenosis means self-emptying. In his Letter to the Philippians, Paul recounts in poetic form Christ's progression from his ineffable glory in heaven to his ignominious death on a Roman cross (2:6–8). In verse 7, translators tells us that Jesus "emptied himself" (*ekenōsen*), and so we equate the theological term *kenosis* with Christ's outpouring of himself in this Godly act. Hauerwas describes this kenotic movement not as God becoming something outside of God's self, but as a revelation of the very nature of the Godhead, a "complete self-emptying made possible by perfect love." In this gesture, we see the divine perfection of "self-giving," emblematic of the pure love from within which it originates.[16] Christ's followers are called to emulate this same undertaking of love.

"It is only through chosen acts of self-emptying...that we are brought into the sphere of Jesus, his life and his power."[17] As Paul profoundly knew, the Christian life includes the life of the cross, and so replication of Christ's kenosis is essential to our spiritual formation. Contemplative prayer facilitates this self-surrender. Bourgeault speaks to the discipline of Centering Prayer as "kenosis in meditation form," because the aim of this open-mindedness is simply release—of thoughts, of emotions, of self—replicating Christ's ministry of the same.[18] However, the kenotic effect of contemplative prayer is not limited to any particular practice. As we have seen in the previous chapter, *all* contemplation that has Christ as its ultimate focal point tends to change the perceptive apparatus of the mind, albeit in differing ways. The "self" prior to contemplation no longer exists—it dies—because that self has been opened up and poured out through prayer. As a result, the experiences that formed the ego and its associated awareness are slowly released, and what remains is the "true" or "God-conscious self."[19]

Self-abandonment is undoubtedly disorienting, and Jesus's echo of the psalmist, "My God, my God, why have you forsaken me?" (Ps 22:1), adequately expresses the depths of the disorientation. The tone and intimacy of this fourth word from the cross speak to a soul that is distressed and unsettled. Yet, within this psalm and others of its type, there is also promise on the horizon.[20] That potential includes a new framework of identity and purpose. But before these can be realized, the old must be discarded.

Kenosis also means reestablishing identity and purpose. When Jesus utters his sixth word, "It is finished" (John 19:30), he signifies completion. It is the end of his ministry. It is the end of his battle with the world. And it is the end of his life. But the work of the cross also indicates the triumphant end of our misperceptions. Athanasius of Alexandria, the fourth-century Church Father, wrote that God "assumed humanity that we might become God. He manifested Himself by means of a body in order that we might perceive the Mind of the unseen Father. He endured shame from men that we might inherit immortality."[21] Through death on the cross, Christ reveals the identity of God as love, and he discloses the true purpose of the Messiah—humanity's access to reconciliation. The words, "It is finished," mark the end of being something or someone we were never intended to be. They mark the end of the delusional life, knowing ourselves as the product of others' opinions and seeing through the clouds of fear and reaction, instead offering a portal of clarity through which we understand life as God intended. The words, "It is finished," allow for unifying change.

In Matthew's Gospel, Jesus tells his disciples, "Truly I tell you, unless you change and become like children, you will never enter the kingdom of heaven" (Matt 18:3). Our understanding of human development sheds valuable light on this rather enigmatic statement. Researchers theorize that little children have a very different sense of "self" relative to adults. In fact, they posit that prior to four months of age, infants see few distinctions between themselves and their primary caregiver.[22] Jesus counsels his followers to reconnect with their "inner child," nullifying the divisive identities they have assumed and awakening to the reality of relational existence with God, their "primary caregiver." Contemplation of life on the cross shows the way.

Contemporary contemplative Beatrice Bruteau understood that even the prayer we attempt is based on how we identify ourselves, an idea that also colors our image of God. For Bruteau, then, the work of prayer becomes a discipline of establishing the proper relational identity.[23] The essence of that work involves erasing the old self or selves to make room for the new:

> As it "loses" each of these "selves," the praying consciousness "finds itself" more and more at liberty. The more you take off bondage, the freer you become; the more you lose restrictions, the vaster you become. The more you empty yourself of predicates, the more you become full of Being. When you are perfectly empty of all predicates...then you are intensely full of pure "I am."[24]

Contemplative prayer provides a method through which this relationality with God is realized. At the center of all Christian contemplation dwells Christ, and we gravitate toward his kenotic identity as we engage in moments of rewiring the mind through intentional active or passive prayer. "It is finished" ends the futility of basing identity and purpose on anything outside of this truth. We identify with Christ, and we assume our natural roles of co-creators with the Divine.[25] Using Clare of Assisi's mirror imagery, Delio puts a fine point on the discussion: "To find oneself in the mirror of the cross is to see the world not from the foot of the cross but from the cross itself. How we see is how we love, and what we love is what we become."[26] But this love remains predicated on death.

Kenosis is the demise of the old self. The final portion we use from Hauerwas's template is Jesus's seventh word, "Father, into your hands I commend my spirit" (Luke 23:46). While this familiar statement invokes images of solace and well-being, it also portends an eerie voyage into the darkness. We remember that these words announce the onset of Good Friday, when we leave a shrouded sanctuary and our only hint of humanity is a lone crown of thorns that adorns an altar or a cross. These words herald a period of silence and mystery.

The sixteenth-century mystic John of the Cross penned the now famous poem "Dark Night," which is a graceful recounting of the Carmelite's experience of contemplation. John also authored an extensive commentary on the poem, opening windows to both his revelation and the theological positions he espoused. The title of this work has become iconic, symbolizing the struggles of the soul related to perceived deprivation of the intellect, memory, and will along the spiritual journey.[27] This "dark night of the soul" is emblematic of the self's demise.

The "darkness" of Good Friday is one through which all Christians must pass. Ours is not simply a journey *up to* the cross, content to sit and mourn an elevated Jesus whose work we appreciate but whose life we dare not imitate. That same

Christ calls the faithful to lose their lives for his sake (cf. Matt 16:25), and this necessitates climbing *upon* the rugged tree, splinters, nails, and all. But as we have seen, that is love's vantage point, and so we "let go and enter into the storm."[28] We intentionally release our will to God, trusting the Divine to navigate the unknown. Symeon understood this type of faithfulness, and he describes its outcome from his own perspective:

> [Whoever] kills his will by effort, with attention and zeal specially directed towards this end, and becomes devoid of will, has obviously transcended his nature and is outside it. Such a man no longer himself wishes anything, since he has no wishes of his own, and does nothing of himself....[29]

Such death, as it relates to self, is *apatheia*, severing all ties to things not related to the attitude of Christ, such as ambitiousness, conceit, or self-interest (Phil 2:3–4).[30] These traits are the treasured possessions of the ego-consciousness, that sense of self that develops over time. But when the ego is eradicated, there is no longer a means of relative experience—including that of God. The spiritual rug gets snatched from under us:

> When [the ego-self falls away] we do indeed feel bereft of the divine and the self, but only the self and divine we knew to this point in the journey.... Thus the falling away of the ego and its immature level of knowing the divine has forced us to go deeper; from experiencing the divine on our own ground (the ego), we must now experience the divine on its own Ground, a Ground where our being or existence takes its life from the divine.... Initially the interior nothingness, darkness and emptiness that takes the place of the self-center

(ego) seems to be nothing but nothing. As it turns out, however, this is the divine, but the divine never before experienced or seen by any ego-self naturally.[31]

The "dark night of the soul" experience described here is a by-product of contemplation. The soul that longs for God and seeks out the Spirit through contemplation interprets the death of the ego-self as the loss of God, since there is no other means by which to interpret that connection. God cannot be perceived in the standard subject/object formation, and therefore, there is no perception at all. Contemplative prayer results in practitioners "rethinking" their perceptions, since their experiences and memories have been short-circuited and then organized anew. Having no contextual background from which to draw, this re-organization is disorienting, and ultimately the one who prays must learn to "re-experience" God afresh from a subject/subject orientation. There is a waiting period, however, and the time between experiences is life within the void, the passage of the "dark night." From the vantage of the cross, we might also call it the "Good Friday effect."

Psalm 22 begins with a cry of desertion. From the cross of Friday to the tomb of late Saturday night, Christ wages war with the forces of disorientation and discontent. He "descends into hell" in a way only God can, plumbing the depths of desolation and despair. But then there is a turn. As with most of the lament psalms, this one too ends on a note of "deliverance" (v. 31; cf. vv. 21–30). Similarly, Jesus arises from his tomb on Sunday, wholly delivered from the cold, dank confines of his "dark night." And so too does the contemplative.

Commentary on John of the Cross's "Dark Night" notes that the "point of arrival to which the night leads is the 'new self,' divinized in being and operation, living now a life of faith, hope, and love, fortified and pure."[32] The Good Friday effect is only temporary; the death of the self is but a rite of passage through which we emerge transformed.

RESURRECTION: CHRIST-LIKE PERCEPTION

Jesus tells Nicodemus that "no one can see the kingdom of God without being born from above" (John 3:3). Nicodemus's confused response reiterates what Christ already knew—an enculturated mind that has not been "rewired" to a new perception cannot possibly see that a changed mind-set is the answer![33] It is just this type of "rebirth" that, given lasting practice and attention, the contemplative undergoes.

As a mystic, Symeon undoubtedly understood this transformational reality. The wisdom he imparts to his monastic audiences and the broader religious community reflects his firsthand experience with emergence in Christ. This judicious excerpt from the *Philokalia* illustrates the breakthrough Symeon realized:

> There is a death which precedes physical death and a resurrection of souls which precedes the resurrection of bodies—by means of deeds, experience, power and truth. For when mortal wisdom is destroyed by immortal mind and death is banished by life, then the soul, as it were risen from the dead, sees itself clearly, as one awakened from sleep, and knows the true God Who has resurrected it.[34]

Clearly, Symeon follows our model: through contemplation, a death of the self that "precedes physical death" and eradicates "mortal wisdom" occurs. After this experience of the cross, a "resurrection of the soul" ensues, replacing previous misperceptions with the "immortal mind" that now "sees itself clearly" in Christ, "the true God who has resurrected it." All of this comes as a gift of the Spirit, predicated on a life of contemplative opening to that Spirit. And this new attitude grounds new behavior.

Jesus hinted at "resurrection seeing" throughout his ministry via parables. In one such story, he alludes to this vision:

> Then the righteous will answer him, "Lord, when was it that we saw you hungry and gave you food, or thirsty and gave you something to drink? And when was it that we saw you a stranger and welcomed you, or naked and gave you clothing? And when was it that we saw you sick or in prison and visited you?" And the king will answer them, "Truly I tell you, just as you did it to one of the least of these who are members of my family, you did it to me." (Matt 25:37–40)

To see as Christ sees has two outcomes that are particularly relevant to our discussion. First, the acts he promotes in this parable—feeding the hungry, giving drink to the thirsty, welcoming the stranger, clothing the naked, tending to the sick, visiting the prisoner—all represent a response to suffering and need. They are acts of *compassion*. Not only is the mind awakened through contemplative work but, as we have seen, it relocates itself in the heart. Second, the opportunities for compassion must be *recognized*, so Jesus attempts to refocus his disciples' vision: "just as you did it to one of the least of these . . . you did it to me." To see someone in need is to see them as part of the Body, not unlike ourselves. Thus, to show compassion necessitates the relational connections of *unitive perception*. Both compassion and unitive vision are derivatives of contemplative prayer.

Compassion

Ilia Delio speaks of two different types of suffering. The first comes from a place of deficiency. In this condition, we have either lost or lack something that is otherwise essential to our personhood, and our integrity is fractured as a result. The second type of suffering comes from sharing out of abundance, *ex abundantia*. Here, we can suffer alongside someone else, sufficient in our own selves and able to give out of love. This giving is how God suffers; and this suffering is known as *compassion*.[35] The resurrection of the new self insists on this form of suffering.

Cast in the image of the Image, we too must love *ex abundantia*. Delio states elsewhere that "to be an image of God is to be relational, to love, to suffer with another and ultimately to lay down one's life for a friend."[36] As is the case with the faithful in general, the post-resurrection self is not free from sin or its ill effects. Christ himself was victimized by the world's injustice, a battered and bruised form on the cross evincing that truth, and he went on to endure the grave and the hellish mystery beyond. Yet it was all done out of compassion, an offering of infinite love poured out for all creation. Understanding the union with Christ's offering for us, the resurrected self replicates this same movement of solidarity. Compassion becomes our "second nature," as living ambassadors for Christ in the world (2 Cor 5:20).[37] Giving of self out of abundance is a by-product of the contemplative heart and mind.

Compassion is essentially about presence, a means of attending to God by attending to others. This intense awareness is nurtured through consistent contemplation. Henri Nouwen terms prayer a "discipline of compassion," a way of practicing presence. Contemplation's central act is attentiveness to the

Spirit, the "bearer of the new mind" that opens us to recognizing the relational bonds of our common experience in God:

> In the intimacy of prayer, God is revealed to us as the God who loves all members of the human family just as personally and uniquely as God loves us. Therefore, a growing intimacy with God deepens our sense of responsibility for others. It evokes in us an always increasing desire to bring the whole world with all its suffering and pains around the divine fire in our heart and to share the revitalizing heat with all who want to come.[38]

In recognizing this truth, we sit in a place of communion with the living Spirit that incarnated and joined our human lot. From this location, our love for others in their mutual suffering—compassion—flowers to its fullest state, and we become agents of God's healing and reconciliation in the world.

In Matthew's account, Jesus states: "You shall love your neighbor as yourself" (22:39). The word "as," here, is typically regarded as an adverb, referring to the extent or degree of the verb "love"—"You shall love your neighbor *in the way or by the amount that you love* yourself." However, it may be just as appropriate for the word "as" to be a preposition, which would present a new interpretation of Jesus's words, "You shall love your neighbor *as if they were you*."[39] This new reading implies a different kind of seeing, one where "neighbor" is no longer an object upon which we operate, but instead we see one another as extensions of our subjective selves.[40] In this context, there are a multitude of mirrors into which we gaze, but a single Image is reflected back from each glass. This unitive vision is essential to compassion, and its cultivation is at the heart of contemplative practice.

Unitive Perception

The creation story in Genesis speaks to a special relationship between God and humanity. We are made in the divine likeness, an image patterned after God's own self (Gen 1:26–27). At one point, we understood that likeness and its implications, and we lived that unitive reality with God, one another, and the natural world. Later, however, our collective memory of our resemblance was lost. Our image of self became fractured, and division and relative identity became normative. But the truth of our origins reminds us that this sacred connectedness—both to Creator and created—nevertheless remains. The reality of our creation in unity must be reclaimed. That reclamation begins with denying the myth of separation and affirming the reconciliation in Christ. Contemplation assists with both.

Martin Laird, a theologian and modern contemplative, debunks the myth that we are separate from the Divine, noting that "union with God is not something that needs to be acquired but realized."[41] While certainly true that we are not of the same *essence* of God, we are nonetheless bound in a Creator-created relationship, eternally ensconced by the reconciling work of Christ. Contemplation allows this truth to emerge and dissolves the filters of misperception. It assists us in peering into the depths of our being, past the emotions and interpretations of distorted memories, and it grounds us in a quiet place that, while ineffable, is where the Spirit enduringly dwells.

Paul understood this permanence. One of the boldest truths that the apostle proclaims in his Letter to the Romans is that *nothing* separates us "from the love of God in Christ Jesus" (Rom 8:39). This love is a unifying force that cannot be overcome by anything creation has to offer. In fact, God's love is so supreme that it *is* our true identity:

Love is not a thing. You are not a thing. You are not a
container that needs to be filled up with love, like a cup
or a bowl or a bucket. When you see completely
through the illusion of self as a fixed entity or thing,
you directly experience that you are not separate from
ultimate reality or God. God is love. You are not separate from God's love. You are God's love.[42]

Recognizing this truth is a gift of the Spirit. We open ourselves to this gift when we work via contemplation to regain the
"pre-Me-self," that child-like mind untethered from precon-
ceived notions of identity and selfhood, an identity clouded by
pain and misperceptions accumulated over time. Freed from
these bonds, we recognize ourselves as the ambassadors of love
we truly are. We participate more fully in the Trinity, itself a mutual indwelling of love that fluidly encapsulates its persons with
no comprehension of beginning or end. We accept our invitation
into that flow, fulfilling the joy of divine perichoresis that was,
and is, and is to come (cf. Rev 1:8).[43] We say "no" to separation,
and we say "yes" to the reconciling work of Christ.

Paul affirms the reality of conversion when he declares that
"it is no longer I who live, but it is Christ who lives in me" (Gal
2:20). He recognizes that his nature is that of Christ, made possible through God's reconciling work in the Incarnate One.
Bound to the Body in this way, Paul is also linked to all others
in that same connection. Merton supports this logic, saying that
the Christian's "inner self is...inseparable from Christ and
hence it is in a mysterious and unique way inseparable from all
the other 'I's' who live in Christ, so that they all form one 'Mystical Person,' which is 'Christ.'"[44]

As we saw in chapter 2, this unity in the Living Word is the
means through which we also obtain oneness with the Father
(cf. John 17:20–23), the formation of a loving community that

weds God and creation. Living the gospel demands a consciousness of this communal wholeness, the ability to imagine the limitless scope of love as it unifies the divine and the finite. It is predicated on knowing our neighbor as Christ, a holy extension of our subjective selves. It compels a relational approach to life, intent on co-creating with God and others to continue the divine work from the beginning, "when God began to create heaven and earth" (Gen 1:1, JPS).[45] It necessitates the formation of a new identity.

When looking at the model of the Trinity, three "persons" in one, the idea of "unique" identity applies only to the whole. God is one, and therefore there exists only one identity of God—we term it "love." Through divine adoption, we share this sacred union. Bruteau provides a thumbnail sketch of this unified landscape:

> The whole question of unique "identity" *at all*—the identity that is "mine" or "yours"—may disappear because "my" identity" is "your" identity is "Christ's" identity, is God's identity. There is an "I," but it is not the "I" that had formerly been meant when "I" was said; rather, where "I" was said, one could now as well say "Christ" (cf. Gal 2:20). And finally, God is all in all (1 Cor 15:28).[46]

In this divine union, we remain "ourselves," yet we at once recognize ourselves in the "other." Seeing holistically does not come naturally. Such perception requires training of both mind and spirit.

Contemplation assists us in this transition. Prayerful practice allows us to intentionally strip away the foundational myths of division, while simultaneously opening us to the reality of Christ's reconciliation. It centers us in Christ, and the mind and the spirit reorient themselves to that true north. With no other reference point, our identities unify with that single focus. The resulting perception is one that understands wholeness and relationality as the ultimate truth, a revival of self united to Christ's ongoing resurrection.

The ideas of Bonaventure provide fertile soil for the seeds of our contemplative death and resurrection thesis to germinate. According to one of his interpreters, this thirteenth-century mystic insists that God's intentions have a circular trajectory, with beginnings and endings intimately entwined:

> Alpha and Omega are finally the same, and the lynchpin holding it all in unity is the "Christ Mystery," or the essential unity of matter and spirit, humanity and divinity. The Christ Mystery is thus the template for all creation, and even more precisely the crucified Christ, who reveals *the necessary cycle of loss and renewal* that keeps all things moving toward ever further life.... [This] pattern is invariably hidden or denied, and therefore must be revealed by God—which is "the cross."[47]

Death is inevitable. But life advancing from that death is likewise expected. That is the profound evolutionary nature of the universe, and God reveals that meaning clearly and finally in the "Christ Mystery." Contemplation plays a function in both this death and its companion of resurrection in the evolution of the human spirit.

ATONEMENT REVISITED

Before we conclude this chapter, the previous discussion prompts a question: If atonement theories are concerned with the work of Christ, specifically the action of the cross, what does our interpretation of these events as presented here contribute to that conversation? In other words, can the death and resurrection of Christ be seriously considered as paving the way for what we might term a *"self-death/identity-resurrection theory,"* one that complements existing atonement concepts? A brief analysis of three prominent models reveals continuities between each and the liberated mind.

The *Christus victor* theory claims that cosmic forces of evil hold humanity captive and bar us from fulfillment in God. Christ defeats these malevolent powers through his death and resurrection, rendering them neutralized in the struggle for human freedom. The *satisfaction* or *substitution* theory holds that humanity owes God a debt because of its sinful response in Adam, a debt that only God's sinlessness can repay. Jesus as the Word made flesh vicariously represents humanity, suffers on its behalf, and in so doing fulfills its obligation. Lastly, the *moral influence* theory of atonement posits that nothing is more powerful than the love of God. To model that cosmic reality, God gives of God's self in the most unconditional way possible, through Incarnation, suffering, and death; the appropriate response to this act of selflessness is awe, gratitude, and replication.[48]

Contemplation results in a synthesis of these three historical theories. As in *Christus victor*, hordes of misperceptions and false identities ensnare us and bar us from true personhood in God. The contemplative wages war on these forces through the process of death to the old self, resurrecting into the new mind and clearing the way for this Godly identification. Similar to Christ's suffering in the satisfaction theory, the contemplative "suffers" through the transition from worldliness to *apatheia*, dying to its affinity for wealth or status or control via kenosis and enduring the Good Friday effect. All is done in the name of discipleship, an "obligation" to pick up the cross daily and imitate Christ (cf. Matt 16:24). Finally, the kenotic act of contemplation replicates the divine self-giving of the moral influence theory, focusing on the work of Christ and modeling his action through self-denial and attentiveness to others through prayer. Self-death/identity-resurrection theory assumes allegorical elements from these three historical models to form something authentically unique.

Each atonement theory is an answer to a slightly different question.[49] For example, the satisfaction/substitution theory provides the answer to the question: "How do I avoid the punishment I deserve due to sin?" However, if the question were: "How can I understand the unconditionality of God's love?" the more appropriate response would be the moral influence theory. Using this same logic, we can see self-death/identity-resurrection taking a place along the spectrum of atonement theories, as it provides an answer to the question: "How do I participate in the redemptive work of creation?"

Recalling Jesus's proclamation "I am the way," the faithful are charged to follow suit. Paul notes that "if we have been united with him in a death like his, we will certainly be united with him in a resurrection like his" (Rom 6:5). We certainly know that Paul understands this death and resurrection to be the *literal* salvific acts of Christ, actions carrying cosmic implications for all creation. But, like Paul and others, we also understand that biblical words and actions can take on layers of meanings, thus the mystery of the Bible itself. So, Paul goes on to address his beloved in Rome that "you too must *think* of yourselves as [being] dead to sin and living for God in Christ Jesus" (Rom 6:11, NAB; emphasis added). Paul implores his audience to adopt a new *perception* of themselves, using Christ's death and resurrection as the model. If we dare, we could take Paul's model one step further.

As it goes for Christ, so it goes for us. Thus, we can envision Christ's death as a death to *his* ego-self, in all the paradoxical majesty that image evokes. And in his resurrection, he reveals humanity's "true nature" as none other than Christ. In other words, *Jesus literally underwent this process of self-death and identity-resurrection* during his work for us.[50] He shows "the way" of passing through the old self to the new, and in fact, mandates that the faithful *must* follow suit. He gives us the path for "at-one-ment," the key to understanding—and attaining—unity with God through himself.

CONCLUSION

There is a cycle of creation to which we all belong. Death is an inevitable reality in that cycle, but it is not the final word. Through Christ's resurrection, we are united in God, enlivened as partakers in the same eternal transformation. The contemplative consciousness experiences this same sequence of events. The "self" dies to the world through *apatheia*, resisting the external stimuli that would coalesce to form misguided perceptions in the mind. Likewise, the contemplative pours out self through voluntary denial of personal gratification or control, opening to the working of the Spirit that makes any transformation possible. After enduring the seeming arid emptiness of the Good Friday event, a rebirth occurs. The contemplative mind is renewed in its identity with a "christic consciousness ... a mind focused on one thing, the centrality of divine love."[51] This renewal frees a fount of compassion born of a total sense of unity with God, neighbor, and even creation at large.

The pattern of Christ's death and resurrection becomes a model for prayer, a template that the contemplative follows for reconciliation. Prayerful atonement emulates Jesus's work, work that "demands that people themselves be rescued from the powers that enslave the world in order that they can in turn be rescuers."[52] This effort aids contemplatives in understanding and orienting themselves in their rightful place in God through Christ.

Paul exhorts the Roman church to remember the pattern of death and life that was preached to them:

> We know that our old self was crucified with him so that the body of sin might be destroyed, and we might no longer be enslaved to sin. For whoever has died is freed from sin. *But if we have died with Christ, we believe that we will also live with him.* We know that Christ, being raised from the dead, will never die again; death no longer has dominion over him. The death he died, he died to sin, once for all; but the life he lives, he lives to God. *So you also must consider yourselves dead to sin and alive to God in Christ Jesus.* (Rom 6:6–11; emphasis added)

The contemplative follows this same path. We die as Christ died, and we likewise rise. We emulate this cycle to move toward the perfection that is ours. It is possible only through the Spirit, yet our efforts are an attempt to abandon our self-will to God, shaping our consciousness to be the same "that was in Christ Jesus" (Phil 2:5).

Conclusion

Several weeks after the prayer study concluded, the pastor encountered one of the participants in the church kitchen. The two had been chatting about various volunteer activities when the conversation turned. As a lady in her early seventies, the parishioner was reevaluating her priorities and how she would dispense her time going forward. She indicated that she would engage in more self-reflection, and then added that she had not suspended her prayer regimen. In fact, she had adapted portions of it to fit her personal prayer style. Of special note was her description of the twenty-third psalm. She was using an Ignatian imagination form of reading the text, and as she walked beside the "still waters" there were three people in the scene—the Shepherd, her, and the pastor! The three would walk for a while at the water's edge, sharing the silence together. Then she would escort the pastor away and continue her journey with the Shepherd. She had fully embraced the notion of contemplative prayer to the point where her imagination was expressing itself in bold, new, inclusive ways. As a result, her place in the world was changing, and her notion of self, others, and God had been reshaped. It had been a long journey, but she was finally experiencing the peace that was—and would eternally be—hers.

As Paul preaches to the Athenians, he speaks of God as one in whom "we live and move and have our being" (Acts 17:28).

This life equates to a full participation in the Divine, a continuous movement of harmony and love. It epitomizes relationship, the Trinity within itself, and the extended community that forms because of God's life-affirming Spirit. It is a unity akin to nuclear fusion, the "binding energy" witnessed as an unshakable force (Rom 8:38–39). But to live into the fullness of this love, we must first know ourselves to be part of this universal whole. That vision requires the synergistic work of people and the Spirit.

Ilia Delio rightly asserts that "Christian life ... requires personal responsibility," and she goes on to explain the disposition of such a believer: "One must desire to put on the mind of Christ, one must *choose* to follow the way of the gospel...."[1] This choice is the expression of free will that we all must accede to on the path of adopting the divine will. It begins with a profession of "yet, not my will but yours be done" (Luke 22:42), and it continues with adopting a life oriented toward habitual Christ-like behavior. Contemplative prayer enables these habits.

THE JOURNEY

Contemplation is a means of discovery. Through contemplation we discover ourselves, we see the world, and we recognize creation in the oneness of God. Contemplation proactively engages the spiritual life that prepares us for the inevitable surprise of the Spirit. John Main expresses the role and character of the contemplative act in these words:

> The call to meditate is an invitation to stop leading our lives on the basis of second-hand evidence. It is a call to each one of us to come to grips with our spiritual capacity and so to discover for ourselves the astonishing richness of the human capacity that is anchored in the divine reality, in the divine life-power. And it is also an

invitation to be simply open to that power, to be ener-
gized by it and to be swept along by it, into the depths
of the divine reality itself.[2]

The contemplative dives headlong into the deep end of the
spiritual life, testing spiritual buoyancy and alternating time between treading sacred water and submerging to the depths of
mystery.

Because all perceptions begin and end in the mind, refram-
ing the consciousness becomes an overtly human act. No different from reading scripture, fasting, or attending to the
sacraments, this work of piety has, as its end, a greater attentiveness to God. As with other devotional acts, contemplation engages known physiological processes responsible for building
and maintaining Christ-like behaviors (e.g. patience, compassion, humility, etc.). We strengthen these processes via intentional practice just as we would fortify our physical selves to
execute the divine mission. Through training the mind, we align
our focus to those "heavenly" ideals that affirm our image in the
divine likeness. All the while, the contemplative fully maintains
that divine revelation and transformation remain the purview of
the Spirit.[3]

As we have noted on several occasions, any encounter with
God is a gift of the Spirit. It cannot be manufactured; it cannot be
coerced. We must prepare ourselves to receive this grace, but it is
nevertheless freely given by God as God sees fit. And to reject the
notion that God does indeed grace some with this gift is contrary
to the biblical witness. Symeon the New Theologian warned
against such belief, undermining the naysayers of his time:

> But to deny that at this present time there are some who
> love God, and that they have been granted the Holy
> Spirit and ... that they have become gods by knowledge
> and experience and contemplation, that wholly sub-

verts the Incarnation of our God and Savior Jesus Christ *(Titus 2:13).*[4]

Symeon knew the Spirit of God as unequivocally the same as the Spirit of Christ, and like his fellow mystics Paul, Bonaventure, and Clare of Assisi, he also understood that humanity has access to that same divine gift through Christ's death and resurrection. To deny that such a state could be attained was to deny God's reconciling work, a condition tantamount to blasphemy. As we see in Symeon's attestation, the work of contemplative prayer serves as an avenue to this spiritual gift—a "means of grace."[5]

Contemplation is indeed a channel through which the human and divine come together for change. The reality of this outcome and its full impact are tangible:

> It is prayer that can change us, make no mistake about it. The changes may go unnoticed for a long time, but they will come. It will change the way we see our work and our rest. It will change the way we live with others. It will slowly, inexorably draw us into itself and unto the One for Whom and by Whom it is prayed, and into the sanctity of the days that have been given us and which we have been given.[6]

Contemplative prayer changes our perceptions. It helps remove the mental clutter so that our true focus—God—becomes clear. This form of prayer moves us toward seeing as Christ saw and as God wills for us to see today, beyond the delusions of divisiveness, scarcity, or injury. It invites us into the deep unity for which Jesus pleads (John 17:21), and it is essential for the healthy functioning of the Body (Eph 4:1–6). Given its vital nature, contemplation must be (re)introduced into the life of the church.

A Note to Clergy and Laity

Henri Nouwen predicted that sometime soon the church would be guilty of failing "at its most basic task: to offer people creative ways to communicate with the divine source of human life," and he saw the central means of this communication as prayer, specifically meditative prayer.[7] Nouwen's dire prediction challenges today's clergy and laity to reevaluate how we encourage and enable this form of spiritual formation.

As we noted at the outset, the notion of prayer has a general connotation of petition and intercession. Most people do engage in contemplative practices—sacred reading, mindfulness, silence, and so forth—but they are unaware of these as named, historically *Christian* traditions. Given that unfamiliarity, there is no intentionality built into their practice. Without rigor, the haphazardness of the prayer method becomes undisciplined, and the result is something increasingly "self-centered and myopic."[8] Education on these methods of approaching the Divine reduces the tendency toward self and opens the person to a world in which he or she finds a practice or group of practices that connect with his or her personality and lifestyle. This openness, in turn, leads to greater creativity in spiritual formation in general, which tends to reinforce this creativity in positive and expansive ways. As the goal is always "contemplation in action," the ultimate outcome is not only self-refinement but also compassionate community engagement. Nevertheless, it all begins with instruction.

Contemplative pedagogical methods can take many forms, but the key is *practice*. Some learners are comfortable in a classroom context, with hands-on, curriculum-based instruction as the primary means of delivery. For others, group prayer retreats in settings that are conducive to quiet and/or engagement with nature are more effective. Still others may prefer one-on-one spiritual direction, the director providing suggestions and guidance suitable to the nuance tolerance of the directee. Regardless of the delivery method—classroom, retreat space, individual—the emphasis must be praxis. *Experiencing* contemplation opens the door to the world of the inner space, a gateway for many that remains obscured by the modern tendency toward "attractional" churches, where worship is the central activity and programmatic content is competitively positioned within a larger marketplace of religious "goods and services" to attract new consumers.[9] The "gateway" of contemplation is overgrown with society's ideas of consumerism. Church leadership needs to clear the brush to these hidden portals (think Narnia and the wardrobe being hidden as the siblings have gotten older).

Education is a process. As with any new learning, it must be reinforced with permanent scaffolding, supplying more layers to assist in the growth process. Maintaining an awareness of, and access to, contemplative practice requires a culture that promotes this prayerful movement as something desirable and indeed necessary. Systemic activities that support such a culture range from preaching about meditation, to engraining *lectio divina* into standard biblical study groups, to full-on contemplative worship times carved out of the weekly schedule. Ultimately, it must grow out of the local parish; the goal, however, is nothing less than the overall mission of the church—an environment where people learn to become disciples with an "alternative imagination" for being the Body of Christ.[10]

Reflecting on contemplative education, theologian David Keller (from whom we borrowed our original definition of contemplation) speaks boldly and concisely to our thesis:

> Contemplative prayer is crucial to the challenges of our era. It is an emptying of self to gain one's self. It is a letting-go of control to become a vessel of reconciliation and transformation. In its rejection of self-interest,

it is totally countercultural, and yet at the same time it is perhaps the single most practical needed thing in the postmodern world. It is also one of the fundamental dimensions of the Christian gospel and way of life.[11]

Contemplation is about self-emptying: a practice of letting go. But in the end, it is all about gain—gain of self, gain of other, gain of God. Contemplative prayer is about seeing the unified connection of Alpha and Omega and the "I" that is "You" that is "Christ" in each other and the world.

Let the same mind be in you that was in Christ Jesus,
who, though he was in the form of God, did not regard
*   equality with God*
as something to be exploited,
but emptied himself,
taking the form of a slave,
being born in human likeness.
And being found in human form,
he humbled himself
and became obedient to the point of death—
even death on a cross.
Therefore God also highly exalted him
and gave him the name
that is above every name,
so that at the name of Jesus
every knee should bend,
in heaven and on earth and under the earth,
and every tongue should confess
that Jesus Christ is Lord,
to the glory of God the Father. (Phil 2:5–11)

Notes

INTRODUCTION

1. Latdict, "precari," http://latin-dictionary.net/definition/31551/precor-precari-precatus, accessed October 13, 2018.
2. Thomas Merton, *Contemplative Prayer* (New York: Image Books, 1969, 1996), 46.
3. "Silent and Solo: How Americans Pray," Barna Group, August 15, 2017, https://www.barna.com/research/silent-solo-americans-pray/.
4. Abhishiktananda, *Prayer* (London: Canterbury Press Norwich, 1967, 2006), 27.
5. Ibid., 36–37.

1. FIRST THINGS

1. Carolyn Osiek, "Philippians," in *The Catholic Study Bible* (Oxford: Oxford University Press, 2006), 476; cf. Morna Hooker, "Philippians," in *The New Interpreter's Bible* (Nashville, TN: Abingdon Press, 2000), 501.
2. Walter Bauer, "φρονέω," in *A Greek-English Lexicon of the New Testament and Other Early Christian Literature* (Chicago: University of Chicago Press, 1979), 866. *Phroneo* is translated as "attitude" in the CEB, NAB, and NIV versions of the text.
3. Fred B. Craddock, *Philippians*, Interpretation: A Bible Commentary for Teaching and Preaching (Louisville, KY: Westminster John Knox Press, 1985), 42–43; cf. Bonnie Thurston and Judith Ryan, *Philippians and Philemon*, Sacra Pagina New

Testament Commentary Series, vol. 10 (Collegeville, MN: Liturgical Press, 2005), 90.

4. Thurston and Ryan emphasize that this type of submissiveness is consistent with a feminist theological interpretation of the text, as this disposition does *not* come as the result of involuntary action or coercion. It is an act of empowerment, suggesting that for something to be given away voluntarily, it first has to be possessed. Thurston and Ryan, *Philippians and Philemon*, 91.

5. Craddock, *Philippians*, 42. Cf. Charles Cousar, *The Letters of Paul*, Interpreting Biblical Texts (Nashville, TN: Abingdon Press, 1996), 139.

6. Bauer, "*νοῦν*," in *A Greek-English Lexicon of the New Testament*, 544.

7. Ibid.

8. Cf. Richard Hays, *First Corinthians*, Interpretation: A Bible Commentary for Teaching and Preaching (Louisville, KY: Westminster John Knox Press, 2011), 45–47.

9. Cf. Cousar, *The Letters of Paul*, 58–62.

10. Ewert Cousins, "Preface to the Series," in *Christian Spirituality, Vol. 1: Origins to the Twelfth Century*, ed. Bernard McGinn, John Meyendorff, and Jean Leclercq (New York: Crossroad, 1987), xiii. Cf. Peter Feldmeier, *Christian Spirituality: Lived Expressions in the Life of the Church* (Winona, MN: Anselm Academic, 2015), 8.

11. Cynthia Bourgeault, *The Heart of Centering Prayer: Nondual Christianity in Theory and Practice* (Boulder, CO: Shambhala Publications, 2016), 55–56; cf. Kallistos Ware, *The Jesus Prayer* (London: Incorporated Catholic Truth Society, 2014), 35; *The Eerdmans Bible Dictionary*, s.v. "heart."

12. Bourgeault, *The Heart of Centering Prayer*, 55. Bourgeault is quoting the Islamic scholar and mystic Kabir Helminski. While the truth of this passage stands on its own, we are sensitive to those readers who may take exception to the words of a non-Christian authority situated within a presumed Christian text. Thus we provide here an excerpt from the Orthodox tradition that resonates with Helminski's sentiment: "The heart, as well as being a physical organ in our chest, represents symbolically the focal point of our personhood as created in the image and likeness of God. The heart is thus the ground of our being, the root and source of our inner

truth. It includes the emotions, but more significantly it comprises our will, our reason, and also the higher visionary faculty known in Greek as the *nous*, whereby we apprehend the glory of God." Ware, *The Jesus Prayer*, 35–36.

13. Bourgeault, *The Heart of Centering Prayer*, 93.

14. Antonio Benítez-Burraco, "How the Language We Speak Affects the Way We Think," *Psychology Today*, https://www.psychologytoday.com/us/blog/the-biolinguistic-turn/201702/how-the-language-we-speak-affects-the-way-we-think. Accessed June 30, 2018.

15. Bourgeault, *The Heart of Centering Prayer*, 153.

16. Ibid., 120.

17. Melissa Joy, "Time Travel through the Eternal Now," https://www.shiftfrequency.com/melissa-joy-jonsson-time-travel-through-the-eternal-now/#more-66732. Accessed September 15, 2017.

18. Bourgeault, *The Heart of Centering Prayer*, 50, 47. Note that this unity of perception should not be confused with the notions of "monism." We do not (nor does Bourgeault) equate nondualism with similar sounding Asian concepts, or what Ken Wilbur frames as "Spirit in 1st-person." Wilbur, *Integral Spirituality* (Boston: Integral Books, 2006), 159; Bernadette Roberts also resists the term "non-duality" in a Christian context because of its implications of monism (and its logical constructs). She argues at length against its use from the perspective of Hinduism in her chapter on "Non-Duality" in her book *The Christian Contemplative Journey: Essays on the Path* (Austin, TX: ContemplativeChristians.com, 2017), 106–31.

19. We do not intend to imply here that Bourgeault does not have this ultimate intention in mind. She clearly states this intent in her essay on Beatrice Bruteau's "Prayer and Identity": "The reason for undergoing this transformation is not personal self-realization or even the personal experience of 'transforming union,' but to be able to participate fully here and now in the generative, kenotic energy of the Trinity...." Bourgeault, "Beatrice Bruteau's 'Prayer and Identity': An Introduction with Text and Commentary," in *Spirituality, Contemplation and Transformation: Writings on Centering Prayer*, ed. Thomas Keating (Brooklyn, NY: Lantern Books, 2008), 113. That spiritual end in mind, this mode of "seeing" is, however, qualitatively aligned with the late A. H. Maslow's notions of "Theory Z." He describes "transcending self-actualizers" as those who

"perceive unitively or sacrally," viewing the world holistically, simultaneously secular and sacred and as one. Maslow, *The Farther Reaches of Human Nature* (New York: Penguin Books, 1971, 1993), 270–86. Maslow also uses the term "unitive perception" directly as the "fusion of the eternal with the temporal, the sacred with the profane." Maslow, *Religions, Values, and Peak Experiences* (New York: Penguin Books, 1970, 1994), 79; cf. 59–96.

20. Evagrius Ponticus, *The Praktikos. Chapters on Prayer*, trans. John Bamberger, Cistercian Studies, vol. 4 (Trappist, KY: Cistercian Publications, 1972), 65.

21. *Westminster Dictionary of Theological Terms*, s.v. "prayer," 216. The fifth-century ascetic John Cassian proposes categories of prayer that also echo our dictionary offering: *petitions, confessions, vows, intercessions,* and *thanksgiving,* a subset of *praise. The Works of John Cassian*, trans. Edgar Gibson (Veritatis Splendor Publications, 2012), 403–7.

22. Walter Brueggemann, *Praying the Psalms: Engaging Scripture and the Life of the Spirit* (Eugene, OR: Cascade Books, 2007), xvi. Cf. Leonardo Boff, *The Lord's Prayer: The Prayer of Integral Liberation* (Maryknoll, NY: Orbis Books, 1983), 5.

23. Hans Urs von Balthasar, *Prayer* (San Francisco: Ignatius Press, 1986), 14.

24. Ibid., 15.

25. Cf. Ray Yungen, *A Time of Departing: How Ancient Mystical Practices Are Uniting Christians with the World's Religions* (Eureka, MT: Lighthouse Trails Publishing, 2010), Kindle edition, loc 526–557. For an in-depth articulation of this view and a counter-argument for contemplation, see John Coe, "The Controversy over Contemplation and Contemplative Prayer: A Historical, Theological, and Biblical Resolution," *Journal of Spiritual Formation and Soul Care* 7, no. 1 (2014): 140–53.

26. George A. Maloney, *Pseudo-Macarius: The Fifty Spiritual Homilies and the Great Letter* (Mahwah, NJ: Paulist Press, 1992), 18.

27. Martin Laird, *Into the Silent Land: The Practice of Contemplation* (New York: Darton, Longman and Todd, 2006), 4.

28. Donald Bloesch, *The Struggle of Prayer* (Colorado Springs: Helmers and Howard, 1988), 154.

29. Namely, whether grace is "imparted" or given by God as some meritorious reward or instead "imputed" vicariously

through the work of Christ without human cause, again devolving into a "works" versus "faith" argument, see Bloesch, *The Struggle of Prayer*, 97–117. For some in opposition, the aversion seemingly betrays vestiges of Reformation-age polemics of Roman Catholic "error" and "heresy"; see David Cloud, "Evangelicals Turning to Catholic 'Spirituality,'" Way of Life Literature, July 30, 2008, last modified September 24, 2019, https://www.wayoflife.org/database/evangelicals_ turning_to_catholic_spirituality.html.

30. Jonathan Edwards, *The Works of Jonathan Edwards, A. M.*, ed. Edward Hickman (London: Ball, Arnold, 1839). Contrary to published accounts (e.g., Bernard McGinn, *The Foundations of Mysticism: Origins to the Fifth Century* [New York: Crossroad, 1991], 269), scrutiny of the work of preeminent theologian Karl Barth also reveals a similar affinity for the "wonders" of the theological endeavor, and specifically as it relates to prayer. Karl Barth, *Evangelical Theology: An Introduction* (Grand Rapids, MI: Wm. B. Eerdmans, 1963), 63–73, 159–170.

31. The "master" here is intended to be God's speech via scripture. The chapter's title, "Silence," indicates the posture of the disciple. Benedict of Nursia, *The Rule of Saint Benedict*, trans. Anthony Meisel and M. L. del Mastro (New York: Doubleday, 1975), 56.

32. John Sommerfeldt, *Bernard of Clairvaux on the Life of the Mind* (Mahwah, NJ: Paulist Press, 2004), 85.

33. John of the Cross, *The Collected Works of St. John of the Cross*, trans. Kieran Kavanaugh and Otilio Rodriguez (Washington, DC: ICS Publications, 1991), 97.

34. While the Western church was developing and refining its versions of *lectio divina*, the Orthodox (Eastern) tradition was simultaneously concerned with sacred *images* as a means of mediating God's presence. These *eikon* (icons) were the visual counterparts to the Holy Text, telling the story of salvation history as worshipers pondered the message they conveyed. In fact, for many the visual representations of figures from the faith tradition conveyed the very presence of God, not unlike the sacramental elements of water and oil or bread and wine. The Orthodox considered these revelations to be no less inspired than the written text itself. As such, these religious icons were not said to be *drawn* (or painted) but *written*. Christine Paintner and Lucy Wynkop, *Lectio Divina: Contemplative*

Awakening and Awareness (New York: Paulist Press, 2008), 121. Cf. Alfredo Tradigo, *Icons and Saints of the Eastern Orthodox Church* (Los Angeles: J. Paul Getty Museum, 2006), 6.

35. The late mystic Henri Nouwen expressed this sentiment eloquently in his work *Discernment: Reading the Signs of Daily Life* (New York: HarperOne, 2013).

36. These "meditations" in Western parlance are akin to the ancient philosopher Marcus Aurelius's musings in *Meditations*, trans. George Long (Mineola, NY: Dover Publications, 1997).

37. M. Basil Pennington, *Centering Prayer: Renewing an Ancient Christian Prayer Form* (New York: Image Books, 2001), 22. The word "ruminate"—to think deeply about something—is rooted in the term "ruminant"—an animal that chews cud (cow, sheep, goat, etc.) and gains nutrients from the fermentation process in a specialized stomach chamber.

38. Ignatius of Loyola, "Particular and Daily Examen," *The Spiritual Exercises*, trans. Elder Mullan (New York: Magisterium Press, 2015). Variations on these daily reflections can be found in Mark Thibodeaux, *Reimagining the Ignatian Examen: Fresh Ways to Pray from Your Day* (Chicago: Loyola Press, 2015).

39. David Keller, "Reading Living Water: The Integral Place of Contemplative Prayer in Christian Transformation," in *Spirituality, Contemplation and Transformation: Writings on Centering Prayer*, ed. Thomas Keating (Brooklyn, NY: Lantern Books, 2008), 132.

40. Harvey Egan, *An Anthology of Christian Mysticism* (Collegeville, MN: Liturgical Press, 1996), 29.

2. UNITIVE PERCEPTION, CONTEMPLATION, AND THE BIBLE

1. Evelyn Underhill, *Mysticism* (New York: Image Books, 1990), 59.

2. Origen, "De Principiis," in *The Complete Works of Origen* (Toronto: 2016), Kindle edition, loc 198. Cf. Harvey D. Egan, *An Anthology of Christian Mysticism* (Collegeville, MN: Liturgical Press, 1996), xxi.

3. We do not use the word "theologian" here completely in the modern sense. Theologians were considered those who experienced God in their daily lives, specifically (but not exclusively)

through prayer. Cf. Hannah Hunt, *A Guide to St. Symeon the New Theologian* (Eugene, OR: Cascade Books, 2015), 107ff. See also William Harmless, *Mystics* (Oxford: Oxford University Press, 2008), 5. Evagrius Ponticus defined this class succinctly in the fourth century: "If you are a theologian you truly pray. If you truly pray you are a theologian." *The Praktikos. Chapters on Prayer*, trans. John Bamberger, Cistercian Studies, vol. 4. (Trappist, KY: Cistercian Publications, 1972), 65.

4. Dionysius the Areopagite, *The Mystical Theology*, trans. C. E. Rolt (Philadelphia: Dalcassian, 2017), 237, Kindle edition.

5. Bernard McGinn, *The Foundations of Mysticism: Origins to the Fifth Century* (New York: Crossroad, 1991), 64.

6. Ibid., 71.

7. T. S. Eliot, *Collected Poems, 1909–1962* (New York: Houghton Mifflin Harcourt, 1963), 154.

8. Isam E. Ballenger, "Ephesians 4:1–16," *Interpretation: A Journal of Bible and Theology* 51, no. 3 (July 1997): 292.

9. Walter Bauer, *A Greek-English Lexicon of the New Testament and Other Early Christian Literature*, 2nd ed. (Chicago: University of Chicago Press, 1979), 267.

10. Walter Brueggemann, *Genesis*, Interpretation: A Bible Commentary for Teaching and Preaching (Atlanta, GA: John Knox Press, 1982), 121.

11. Cf. D. P. Senior and Daniel Harrington, *1 Peter, Jude and 2 Peter*, Sacra Pagina New Testament Commentary Series, vol. 15 (Collegeville, MN: Liturgical Press, 2003), 61–62. Exodus 19:6 reads, "but you shall be for me a priestly kingdom and a holy nation," and Isaiah 43:20–21 states, "my chosen people, the people whom I formed for myself." It seems the author is calling upon these known Judaic references to help his audience understand themselves as part of this same biblical tradition.

12. Ibid., 62.

13. Gerard Sloyan, *John*, Interpretation: A Bible Commentary for Teaching and Preaching (Louisville, KY: Westminster John Knox Press, 2009), 197.

14. Francis Moloney, *John*, Sacra Pagina New Testament Commentary Series, vol. 4 (Collegeville, MN: Liturgical Press, 1998), 474.

15. Ibid., 467.

16. Cf. Gerald F. Hawthorne, Ralph Martin, and Daniel Reid, eds., *Dictionary of Paul and His Letters* (Downers Grove, IL: Inter-Varsity Press, 1993), 433–36.

17. Scholars like John Randall argue that the theme of unity is inseparable from a discussion on the Eucharist. "The Theme of Unity in John 17:20–23," *Ephemerides Theologicae Lovanienses* 41 (January 1965): 373–94.

18. *Strong's Greek Lexicon*, s.v. "*eirēnē*," https://www.blue letterbible.org/lang/lexicon/lexicon.cfm?t=kjv&strongs=g1515, accessed July 2, 2018.

19. Ballenger, "Ephesians 4:1–16," 294.

20. Commission on World Mission and Evangelism, World Council of Churches, "Towards Common Witness to Christ Today: Mission and Visible Unity of the Church," *International Review of Mission* 99, no. 1 (2010): 103.

21. John of Damascus, *Saint John of Damascus: Writings*, trans. Frederic Chase (Ex Fontibus Company, 2015), 202. Cf. Charles Twombly, *Perichoresis and Personhood: God, Christ, and Salvation in John of Damascus* (Eugene, OR: Pickwick Publications, 2015), 8.

22. Susan Davies, "Relational Unity in Mission: Reflecting God's Life," *Journal of Ecumenical Studies* 45, no. 2 (2010): 242.

23. Ballenger, "Ephesians 4:1–16," 294.

24. Ignatius of Loyola, "First Annotation," in *The Spiritual Exercises*, trans. Elder Mullan (New York: Magisterium Press, 2015).

25. Ilia Delio, *Making All Things New: Catholicity, Cosmology, Consciousness* (Maryknoll, NY: Orbis Books, 2015), 161.

26. Mother Teresa, *In the Heart of the World: Thoughts, Stories and Prayers* (Novato, CA: New World Library, 1997), 9.

27. Ibid., 7.

28. Delio, *Making All Things New*, 156.

29. John of the Cross, *The Collected Works of St. John of the Cross*, trans. Kieran Kavanaugh and Otilio Rodriguez (Washington, DC: ICS Publications, 1991), 92.

30. Claus Westermann, *Praise and Lament in the Psalms* (Atlanta, GA: John Knox Press, 1965, 1981), 253.

31. Cf. Henri Nouwen, *Spiritual Formation: Following the Movements of the Spirit* (New York: HarperOne, 2010), xvii.

32. Bauer, *Greek-English Lexicon*, 388.

33. Nouwen, *Spiritual Formation*, xvii.

34. Delio, *Making All Things New*, 158.

35. Bernadette Roberts, *What Is Self? A Study of the Spiritual Journey in Terms of Consciousness* (Boulder, CO: Sentient Publications, 2005), 67.

36. John Kenney, *The Mysticism of Saint Augustine: Rereading the Confessions* (New York: Routledge, 2005), 126.

37. Meister Eckhart, *True Hearing*, trans. Claud Field (Grand Rapids, MI: Christian Classics Ethereal Library, n.d.). http://www.ccel.org/ccel/eckhart/sermons.html, accessed November 24, 2017.

38. Richard B. Hays, *First Corinthians*, Interpretation: A Bible Commentary for Teaching and Preaching (Louisville, KY: Westminster John Knox Press, 2011), 47.

3. The Witness of a Mystic

1. William Harmless, *Mystics* (New York: Oxford University Press, 2008), 5.

2. Hannah Hunt, *A Guide to St. Symeon the New Theologian* (Eugene, OR: Cascade Books, 2015), 2–3. Cf. Niketas Stethatos, *The Life of Saint Symeon the New Theologian*, trans. Richard Greenfield (Cambridge, MA: Harvard University Press, 2013), 5–9; George A. Maloney, *The Mystic of Fire and Light: St. Symeon, the New Theologian* (Denville, NJ: Dimension Books, 1975), 19–24.

3. Harvey Egan, *An Anthology of Christian Mysticism* (Collegeville, MN: Liturgical Press, 1996), 145. Cf. *Symeon the New Theologian: The Discourses*, trans. C. J. de Catanzaro (Mahwah, NJ: Paulist Press, 1980), 1; Jim McInnes, "Theodidact: Symeon the New Theologian's Claim to Be Taught by God," *Journal of Medieval Religious Cultures* 38, no. 2 (2012): 195.

4. The title "Theologian" had been applied only to John the Evangelist and Gregory Naziansus prior to Symeon. Hunt, *Guide*, 108. Cf. *Symeon: The Discourses*, 4; Egan, *Anthology*, 144.

5. Maloney, *The Mystic*, 14. Cf. Hilarion Alfeyev, *St. Symeon the New Theologian and Orthodox Tradition*, Oxford Early Christian Studies (Oxford: Oxford University Press, 2000), 255–69.

6. *Symeon: The Discourses*, "Discourse 24," 262. Cf. Alfeyev, *St. Symeon*, 49–52.

7. Alfeyev, *St. Symeon*, 277. Cf. Hunt, *Guide*, 66–67; Egan, *Anthology*, 311. For comparative study in use and defense of Symeon's ideas, see Gregory Palamas, *The Triads*, trans. John Meyendorff (New York: Paulist Press, 1983).

8. Paul coins the term θεοδίδακτος (*theodidaktos*) in 1 Thess 4:9: "Now concerning love of the brothers and sisters, you do not need to have anyone write to you, for you yourselves have been *taught by God* to love one another" (emphasis added). McInnes, "Theodidact," 197. Cf. Maloney, *The Mystic*, 14. For an extended view on the epistemology of Symeon's approach, see William Abraham, "Symeon the New Theologian," in *The Oxford Handbook of the Epistemology of Theology*, ed. William Abraham and Frederick Aquino (Oxford: Oxford University Press, 2017), 383–92.

9. Stethatos, *Life*, 13.

10. Maloney, *The Mystic*, 14. Cf. Egan, *Anthology*, 145.

11. George A. Maloney, introduction to *Symeon the New Theologian: The Discourses*, 15. Cf. Egan, *Anthology*, 146; Maloney, *The Mystic*, 28; John McGuckin, "Symeon the New Theologian's Hymns of Divine Eros: A Neglected Masterpiece of the Christian Mystical Tradition," *Spiritus: A Journal of Christian Spirituality* 5, no. 2 (2005): 185.

12. *Symeon: The Discourses*, "Discourse 9," 156.

13. Ibid., "Discourse 33," 343.

14. *Symeon the New Theologian: Hymns of Divine Love,* trans. George A. Maloney (Denville, NJ: Dimension Books, 1976), 142.

15. Ibid., 145–46.

16. Ibid., 145. These lines also hint at the arguments that Symeon and his contemporaries engaged in around the contemplative life and universal access to the Holy Spirit, as well as the possibility of becoming a *theodidact*. This "controversy" and others contributed to Symeon's subsequent exile by Byzantine religious authorities. For more, see Stethatos, *Life*, 167–217; cf. *Symeon: The Discourses*, 9–10.

17. E. Kadloubovsky and G. E. H. Palmer, eds., *Writings from the Philokalia on Prayer of the Heart* (London: Faber and Faber, 1951, 1992), 97–142.

18. *Symeon: Hymns*, 122, 116.

19. Ibid., 132.

20. Evagrius Ponticus, *The Praktikos. Chapters on Prayer*, trans. John Bamberger (Trappist, KY: Cistercian Publications, 1972), lxxxiii–iv. This view was not unique to Evagrius, as his predecessors—namely Origen and Gregory of Nyssa—viewed the contemplative life in a similar manner. See Bernard McGinn, *The Foundations of Mysticism: Origins to the Fifth Century* (New York: Crossroad, 1991), 144–57. Cf. Egan, *Anthology*, 43–48.

21. Kadloubovsky and Palmer, *Philokalia*, 107.

22. Ibid., 114–15.

23. Ibid., 137.

24 Maloney, *The Mystic*, 182. Cf. McGuckin, "Symeon," 198.

25. *Symeon: The Discourses*, "Discourse 25," 270.

26. Ibid., 272.

27. Symeon's Discourse 2 is titled "To Christ through the Beatitudes," setting the tone for the rest of the work. *Symeon: The Discourses*, "Discourse 2," 47–59; cf. 104, 111, 160, 185, etc. See also Maloney, *The Mystic*, 141–45; McInnes, "Theodidact," 203; Kadloubovsky and Palmer, *Philokalia*, 122.

28. *Symeon: The Discourses*, "Discourse 31," 332.

29. Kadloubovsky and Palmer, *Philokalia*, 115.

30. Stethatos, *Life*, 11. Cf. *Symeon: The Discourses*, "Discourse 22," 243–45. Note that in *The Discourses*, Symeon often tells his own story via the third-person character named "George"—Symeon's birth name.

31. Stethatos, *Life*, 17–19.

32. *Symeon: The Discourses*, "Discourse 25," 272.

33. Ibid., 159.

34. *Symeon: Hymns*, 67.

35. Maloney, *The Mystic*, 212; cf. 83–111, esp. 105.

36. *Symeon: The Discourses*, "Discourse 2," 58.

37. "Lord Jesus Christ, Son of God, have mercy on me." Cf. *Symeon: The Discourses*, "Discourse 22," 245; "Discourse 30," 322.

38. *Symeon: The Discourses*, "Discourse 33," 340.

39. *Symeon: Hymns*, "Hymn 24," 126.

40. McInnes, "Theodidact," 203.

41. Evagrius, *Praktikos*, 56. Cf. *Symeon: The Discourses*, "Discourse 29," 315; Maloney, *The Mystic*, 129–37; Egan, *Anthology*, 147.

42. *Symeon: Hymns*, 61.

43. *Symeon: The Discourses*, "Discourse 4," 81, cf. 83; "Discourse 9," 159–60. In Discourse 30 Symeon gives a brief explanation of ways in which these tears of contrition may be brought about, including repetition of "Holy, Holy, Holy," the Lord's Prayer, and the Jesus Prayer, and assumption of various physical and mental postures, as well as self-castigation "violently and unsparingly," 322–23. See also the biographical account of Symeon's tears in Stethatos, *Life*, 71, 93.

44. *Symeon: The Discourses*, "Discourse 4," 81–82.

45. Kadloubovsky and Palmer, *Philokalia*, 114. John Climacus, who certainly had a significant influence on Symeon, terms this duality *penthos*—"joy-sorrow"—in the seventh step of his *Ladder*. John Climacus, *The Ladder of Divine Ascent* (Toronto: Patristic Publishing, 2017), 42–49. Cf. Hunt, *Guide*, 88. John of the Cross presents a similar idea on the two-pronged nature of sorrow and tears in his commentary on the first two verses of the first stanza of "Dark Night." John of the Cross, *The Collected Works of St. John of the Cross*, trans. Kieran Kavanaugh and Otilio Rodriguez (Washington, DC: ICS Publications, 1991), 416–28.

46. *Symeon: Hymns*, 44.

47. *Symeon: The Discourses*, "Discourse 4," 88.

48. Maloney, *The Mystic*, 145. Cf. McGuckin, "Symeon," 196–97.

49. Abraham, "Symeon the New Theologian."

50. Kadloubovsky and Palmer, *Philokalia*, 108. Cf. Gal 5:1.

51. *Symeon: Hymns*, 56. Cf. *Symeon: The Discourses*, "Discourse 5," 117–18.

52. "White martyrs" were those who, according to early church writers like Cyprian of Carthage, did not sacrifice their lives for the faith ("red martyrs"), but instead "died daily," like Paul (1 Cor 15:31), to the cares of the world. See Isabelle Kinnard, "*Imitatio Christi* in Christian Martyrdom and Asceticism: A Critical Dialogue," in *Asceticism and Its Critics: Historical Accounts and Comparative Perspectives*, ed. Oliver Freiberger (Oxford: Oxford University Press, 2006), 131–52. Cf. Timothy Ware, *The Orthodox Church* (London: Penguin Books, 1963, 1997), 14–15.

53. Evagrius, *Praktikos*, 34.

54. Kadloubovsky and Palmer, *Philokalia*, 137. This state is similar to the founder of Methodism's controversial notions of

"perfection." John Wesley saw these faithful not as sinless, per se, but so deeply consumed by the love of God that the occasion of sin has no foothold. John Wesley, "Christian Perfection," in *John Wesley's Sermons: An Anthology*, ed. Albert Outler and Richard Heitzenrater (Nashville, TN: Abingdon Press, 1991), 70–84. See also the witness of the anonymous author of *The Cloud of Unknowing*, trans. Ira Progoff (New York: Delta Books, 1957), 90–91.

55. Maloney, *The Mystic*, 152.

56. *Symeon: The Discourses*, "Discourse 28," 299. Cf. Hunt, *Guide*, 71; Kadloubovsky and Palmer, *Philokalia*, 139.

57. Gregory is translated to say that it is on "those of us who continue in this quiet and peaceful course of life that the truth will shine, illuminating the eyes of our soul with its own rays. This truth, which was then manifested by the ineffable and mysterious illumination which came to Moses, is God." Gregory of Nyssa, *The Life of Moses*, trans. Abraham Malherbe and Everette Ferguson (New York: Paulist Press, 1978), 59.

58. *Symeon: Hymns*, 122.

59. *Symeon: The Discourses*, "Discourse 16," 200.

60. Ibid., 202–3. In the "Precepts," Symeon states that if a person looks at the sun, it changes his or her vision. Likewise, when people stare into the "sun of truth with mind and heart," they experience a change in their mental vision, "unable to imagine anything earthly," seeing "God in all things," 141.

61. *Symeon: The Discourses*, "Discourse 36," 376.

62. *Symeon: Hymns*, 254.

63. *Symeon: The Discourses*, "Discourse 34," 350.

64. Ibid., "Discourse 9," 160. Symeon's language here and elsewhere is reminiscent of Augustine's view of contemplation—all is seen properly through the Spirit: "And since [a person] now has the capacity to understand, you teach him [or her] to contemplate the Trinity in Unity, the Unity that is Trinity." Augustine of Hippo, *The Confessions*, trans. Maria Boulding (Hyde Park, NY: New City Press, 1997, 2016), 294. See also John Kenney, *The Mysticism of Saint Augustine: Rereading the Confessions* (New York: Routledge, 2005), 126–27.

65. *Symeon: The Discourses*, "Discourse 32," 335–38.

66. *Symeon: Hymns*, 28.

67. McGuckin, "Symeon," 188. This constant purgation contrasts with the typical threefold, iterative view of purgation, illumination, and union. Others saw these as "overlapping stages," but Symeon construed purification as a necessity throughout the process. On the three stages of purgation, illumination, and union, see Evelyn Underhill, *Mysticism* (New York: Image Books, 1990), 169–70.

68. *Symeon: The Discourses*, "Discourse 22," 245–46.

4. The Contemplative Brain

1. Kathleen Stassen Berger, *The Developing Person: Through the Life Span* (New York: Worth Publishers, 2008), 136. Cf. Allan Combs and Stanley Krippner, "Spiritual Growth and the Evolution of Consciousness: Complexity, Evolution, and the Farther Reaches of Human Nature," *International Journal of Transpersonal Studies* 18, no. 1 (1999): 18.

2. Andrew Newberg, Eugene D'Aquili, and Vince Rause, *Why God Won't Go Away: Brain Science and the Biology of Belief* (New York: Ballantine Books, 2001), 33.

3. Michael S. Sweeney, *Brain: The Complete Mind* (Washington, DC: National Geographic Society, 2009), 10–22. Cf. Oshin Vartanian and Vinod Goel, "Neural Correlates of Creative Cognition," in *Evolutionary and Neurocognitive Approaches to Aesthetics, Creativity and the Arts*, ed. Colin Martindale, et al. (Amityville, NY: Baywood Publishing, 2007), 195–207; Newberg, D'Aquili, and Rause, *Why God Won't Go Away*, 19–22; Shelley Carson, *Your Creative Brain* (San Francisco: Jossey-Bass, 2010), 39–54.

4. Newberg, D'Aquili, and Rause, *Why God Won't Go Away*, 33. For an in-depth discussion of the mind-brain debate, see Jeffrey Schwartz and Sharon Begley, *The Mind and the Brain: Neuroplasticity and the Power of Mental Force* (New York: Regan-Books, 2002), 21–53. Cf. Rick Hanson and Richard Mendius, *Buddha's Brain: The Practical Neuroscience of Happiness, Love, and Wisdom* (Oakland, CA: New Harbinger Publications, 2009), 9–10.

5. Newberg, D'Aquili, and Rause, *Why God Won't Go Away*, 24–32. See also Carson, *Your Creative Brain*, 52–53. Cf. Sweeney,

Brain, 102–3. We should also note that the senses do not seem to operate autonomously, but instead are part of the "additional inputs" that any particular sense receives as well. These come together to help form a "total" sensory picture. Cf. Sweeney, *Brain*, 130–32.

6. Sweeney, *Brain*, 22.

7. Ibid., 177. Cf. Mario Beauregard and Denyse O'Leary, *The Spiritual Brain: A Neuroscientist's Case for the Existence of the Soul* (New York: HarperOne, 2007), 63.

8. For a technically detailed overview of the ANS, see Gerard Tortora and Bryan Derrickson, *Principles of Anatomy and Physiology* (Hoboken, NJ: John Wiley & Sons, 2014), 524–26. Cf. David Robertson et al., eds., *Primer on the Autonomic Nervous System* (Waltham, MA: Academic Press, 2012), Kindle edition, loc 1099–441; J. Allan Hobson, *The Chemistry of Conscious States: How the Brain Changes Its Mind* (Boston: Little, Brown, 1994), 184–86.

9. David Hartman and Diane Zimberoff, "Higher Stages of Human Development," *Journal of Heart-Centered Therapies* 11, no. 2 (2008): 77. Cf. Newberg, D'Aquili, and Rause, *Why God Won't Go Away*, 40–42. Hartman and Zimberoff also describe a fifth state, *hyperquiescence/hyperarousal*, as an experience of oneness.

10. Visual meditation and contemplation are grouped into practices termed *visio divina*—"divine seeing." Repetitive prayers may include myriad methods, such as praying the rosary or reciting the Jesus Prayer ("Lord Jesus Christ, Son of God, have mercy upon me"). Techniques like Ignatius Loyola's *Examen* represent those of self-reflection.

11. Newberg, D'Aquili, and Rause, *Why God Won't Go Away*, 117. For many neurological studies, "active" contemplation is classified as *focused attention monitoring* (FAM), while "passive" techniques are termed *open monitoring meditation* (OMM). Cf. Dominique Lippelt, Bernhard Hommel, and Lorenzo Colzato, "Focused Attention, Open Monitoring and Lovingkindness Meditation: Effects on Attention, Conflict Monitoring, and Creativity—A Review," *Frontiers in Psychology* 5, 1083 (September 2014): 1–5.

12. Newberg, D'Aquili, and Rause, *Why God Won't Go Away*, 120–23.

13. *Symeon the New Theologian: The Discourses*, trans. C. J. de Catanzaro (Mahwah, NJ: Paulist Press, 1980), "Discourse 22," 245–46.

14. Ware calls repetition of the prayer "fixed use" when "we repeat the Jesus Prayer as part of our appointed times for prayer, when our *whole attention is concentrated on the act of praying*" (emphasis added). Kallistos Ware, *The Jesus Prayer* (London: Incorporated Catholic Truth Society, 2014), 15.

15. In comparing this text with Symeon's works like "Hymn 25," he often prayed under "the light of a lamp." His constant imagery of flame and light contributed to the nickname given to him by George Maloney, "Mystic of Fire and Light." *Symeon the New Theologian: Hymns of Divine Love,* trans. George A. Maloney (Denville, NJ: Dimension Books, 1976), "Hymn 25," 135–38. This experience of light is also common to near-death experiences. Author Brian Bain's assessment of a common view from the scientific community is worth reprinting here: "Scientists and academics have not generally accepted the near death experience as an encounter with the Divine by a 'soul' that survives death. In fact, a fairly extensive critical literature has developed contending the contrary, though not all the critics agree on what the cause of the experience might be. Theories range from the influence of an unusual flow of brain chemicals; to the reaction of the dying brain to reduced levels of oxygen; or to purely psychological factors such as dreams, hallucinations, or wish fulfillment. While all of these criticisms offer interesting possibilities, none of them rise above the level of speculation." Brian Bain, "The Divine Light and Ecstasy in Religious and Near-Death Experiences: A Retrospective Glance and a View for the Future," *Journal of Near-Death Studies* 24, no. 4 (2006): 200.

16. Newberg, D'Aquili, and Rause, *Why God Won't Go Away*, 117–19.

17. E. Kadloubovsky and G. E. H. Palmer, eds., *Writings from the* Philokalia *on Prayer of the Heart* (London: Faber and Faber, 1951, 1992), 132.

18. George A. Maloney, *The Mystic of Fire and Light: St. Symeon, the New Theologian* (Denville, NJ: Dimension Books, 1975), 9.

19. Andrew Newberg et al., "Cerebral Blood Flow during Meditative Prayer: Preliminary Findings and Methodological Issues,"

Perceptual Motor Skills 97 (2003): 625–30. The techniques as Newberg et al. describe them in their technical paper actually do not conform to the contemplative practice of Centering Prayer as outlined by Thomas Keating, William Meninger, and the late M. Basil Pennington (cf. M. Basil Pennington, *Centering Prayer: Renewing an Ancient Christian Prayer Form* [New York: Image Books, 2001]). Strangely, Newberg changes the story slightly and *does* lay out an accurate description of Centering Prayer when referencing the experiment in a later book (Andrew Newberg and Mark Waldman, *How God Changes Your Brain: Breakthrough Findings from a Leading Neuroscientist* [New York: Ballantine Books, 2009], 193–95).

20. Newberg and Waldman, *How God Changes Your Brain*, 49.

21. Mario Beauregard and Vincent Paquette, "Neural Correlates of a Mystical Experience in Carmelite Nuns," *Neuroscience Letters* 405 (2006): 186–90. Cf. Beauregard and O'Leary, *The Spiritual Brain*, 255–78. Richer sources of data exist from research with Buddhist contemplatives as the subjects. Avenues of inquiry range from physiological changes to the body to the relationship between mental energy and quantum physics; cf. the works of B. Alan Wallace, *Hidden Dimensions: The Unifications of Physics and Consciousness* (New York: Columbia University Press, 2007), or *Contemplative Science: Where Buddhism and Neuroscience Converge* (New York: Columbia University Press, 2007); or likewise Daniel Goleman and Richard Davidson, *Altered Traits: Science Reveals How Meditation Changes Your Mind, Brain, and Body* (New York: Avery, 2017).

22. Charlotte Tomaino, *Awakening the Brain: The Neuropsychology of Grace* (New York: Atria Books, 2012), 60.

23. Schwartz and Begley, *The Mind and the Brain*, 15. See also Sharon Begley, *The Plastic Mind* (London: Constable and Robinson, 2009). Cf. Daniel Goleman, *Destructive Emotions: How Can We Overcome Them?* (New York: Bantam Books, 2003), 285.

24. Schwartz and Begley, *The Mind and the Brain*, 225–36.

25. Newberg and Waldman, *How God Changes Your Brain*, 48.

26. Jessica Andrews-Hanna, "The Brain's Default Network and Its Adaptive Role in Internal Mentation," *Neuroscientist* 18,

no. 3 (2012): 251–70; Oshin Vartanian, "Attention, Cognitive Flexibility, and Creativity: Insights from the Brain," in *Creativity and Reason in Cognitive Development*, ed. James Kaufman and John Baer (New York: Cambridge University Press, 2016), 246–58.

27. Joon Hwan Jang et al., "Increased Default Mode Network Connectivity Associated with Meditation," *Neuroscience Letters* 487, no. 3 (2011): 358–62. Cf. Judson Brewer et al., "Meditation Experience Is Associated with Differences in Default Mode Network Activity and Connectivity," *Proceedings of the National Academy of Sciences of the United States of America* 108, no. 50 (2011): 20254–59.

28. Brewer et al., "Meditation Experience." Cf. Veronique Taylor, Veronique Daneault, Joshua Grant, et al., "Impact of Meditation Training on the Default Mode Network during a Restful State," *Social Cognitive and Affective Neuroscience* 8, no. 1 (2013): 4–14; Jang et al., "Increased Default Mode."

29. Carson, *Your Creative Brain*, 76.

30. Ibid., 105.

31. Ibid., 96–97.

32. Ibid., 106.

33. Ibid., 108, 112. Cf. Paul Gilbert, *The Compassionate Mind* (London: Robinson, 2013), 204–12.

34. *Your Creative Brain*, 117–18.

35. Ignatius of Loyola, *The Spiritual Exercises*, trans. Elder Mullan (New York: Magisterium Press, 2015).

36. William Abraham, "Symeon the New Theologian," in *The Oxford Handbook of the Epistemology of Theology*, ed. William Abraham and Frederick Aquino (Oxford: Oxford University Press, 2017).

37. Mihaly Csikszentmihalyi, *Flow: The Psychology of Optimal Experience* (New York: Harper Perennial Modern Classics, 2008), 6.

38. Mihaly Csikszentmihalyi, *Creativity: The Psychology of Discovery and Invention* (New York: Harper Perennial Modern Classics, 2013), 110–13. Cf. Indre Viskontas and Bruce Miller, "Art and Dementia: How Degeneration of Some Brain Regions Can Lead to New Creative Impulses," in *Neuroscience of Creativity*, ed. Oshin Vartanian, Adam S. Bristol, and James C. Kaufman (Cam-

bridge, MA: MIT Press, 2013), 126. These nine conditions intersect with Maslow's eighteen descriptions of persons engaged in "peak experience." Abraham Maslow, *The Farther Reaches of Human Nature* (New York: Penguin Books, 1971, 1993), 61–68.

39. Allan Combs and Stanley Krippner, "Structures of Consciousness and Creativity: Opening the Doors of Perception," in *Everyday Creativity and New Views of Human Nature: Psychological, Social, and Spiritual Perspectives*, ed. Ruth Richards (Washington, DC: American Psychological Association, 2007), 143–44.

40. Csikszentmihalyi, *Flow*, 33.

41. This argument aligns with Maslow's notions of the "B-realm" (transcendent) meshing with the "D-realm" (profane). Abraham Maslow, *Religions, Values, and Peak Experiences* (New York: Penguin Books, 1970, 1994), 79.

42. Allan Combs and Stanley Krippner, "Process, Structure, and Form: An Evolutionary Transpersonal Psychology of Consciousness," *International Journal of Transpersonal Studies* 22, no. 1 (2003), 54.

43. Maslow, *Religions, Values, and Peak Experiences*, 62.

44. Cynthia Bourgeault, *The Heart of Centering Prayer: Nondual Christianity in Theory and Practice* (Boulder, CO: Shambhala Publications, 2016), 178.

45. Csikszentmihalyi, *Flow*, 103–4. We should note that the rigor at the top of his list is that of Hatha Yoga, a generic grouping of old-style yoga techniques. See Richard Rosen, *Original Yoga: Rediscovering Traditional Practices of Hatha Yoga* (Boston, MA: Shambhala Publications, 2012).

46. Combs and Krippner, "Spiritual Growth," 19. Cf. Hanson and Mendius, *Buddha's Brain*, 191–204; Tomaino, *Awakening the Brain*, 151. Bourgeault notes that practices akin to Centering Prayer behave as a kind of "apophatic psychotherapy." Cynthia Bourgeault, *Centering Prayer and Inner Awakening* (Lanham, MD: Cowley Publications, 2004), 95ff.

47. Newberg, D'Aquili, and Rause, *Why God Won't Go Away*, 150.

48. Matthew Fox, *Creativity: Where the Divine and the Human Meet* (New York: Tarcher/Putnam, 2002), 28.

49. Fox, *Creativity*, 64. Thomas Merton echoes this sentiment. He notes that the "important thing in contemplation is not

gratification and rest, but *awareness, life, creativity, and freedom.* In fact, contemplation is man's highest and most essential spiritual activity" (emphasis added). Thomas Merton, *The Inner Experience: Notes on Contemplation* (New York: HarperOne, 2003), 34.

50. Aviva Berkovich-Ohana, Joseph Glicksohn, and Tal Dotan Ben-Soussan, "Creativity Is Enhanced by Long-Term Mindfulness Training and Is Negatively Correlated with Trait Default-Mode-Related Low-Gamma Inter-Hemispheric Connectivity," *Mindfulness* 8, no. 3 (2017): 717–27. Cf. Lorenzo Colzato, Ayca Ozturk, and Bernhard Hommel, "Meditate to Create: The Impact of Focused-Attention and Open-Monitoring Training on Convergent and Divergent Thinking," *Frontiers in Psychology* 3, no. 116 (2012): 1–5; Roy Horan, "The Neuropsychological Connection between Creativity and Meditation," *Creativity Research Journal* 21, no. 2–3 (2009): 199–222.

51. Lorenzo Colzato et al., "Meditate to Create." Cf. Amy Wachholtz and Kenneth Pargament, "Is Spirituality a Critical Ingredient of Meditation? Comparing the Effects of Spiritual Meditation, Secular Meditation, and Relaxation on Spiritual, Psychological, Cardiac, and Pain Outcomes," *Journal of Behavioral Medicine* 28, no. 4 (August 2005): 369–84. https://doi: 10.1007/s10865-005-9008-5.

52. Ruth Richards, "Twelve Potential Benefits of Living More Creatively," in *Everyday Creativity and New Views of Human Nature: Psychological, Social, and Spiritual Perspectives*, ed. Ruth Richards (Washington, DC: American Psychological Association, 2007), 289–319.

53. Ibid., 290.

54. Ibid., 291. Cf. "The continual consolidation, revision, 'sculpting,' of the 'attractor' modes of the brain conferred by the preparation of the Christian ultimately confers the daily renewal of life and a 'new mode of living.'" Douglas Anderson, "Neuroscience," in *The Wiley-Blackwell Companion to Christian Mysticism*, ed. Julia Lamm (Malden, MA: John Wiley & Sons, 2012), 662. http://ebookcentral.proquest.com/lib/bridwell/detail.action?docID=1017176, accessed September 17, 2018.

55. Schwartz and Begley, *The Mind and the Brain*, 26.

56. Newberg, D'Aquili, and Rause, *Why God Won't Go Away*, 155.

57. Andrew Newberg, *Neurotheology: How Science Can Enlighten Us about Spirituality* (New York: Columbia University Press, 2018). This field of study is similar to Mario Beauregard's "spiritual neuroscience" in Beauregard and Paquette, "Neural Correlates," and to Charlotte Tomaino's "contemplative neuroscience" in Tomaino, *Awakening the Brain*, 78.

5. THE MIND OF CHRIST

1. Gail O'Day, "John," *The New Interpreter's Bible* (Nashville, TN: Abingdon Press, 1995), 742. Cf. Francis Moloney, *John*, Sacra Pagina New Testament Commentary Series, vol. 4 (Collegeville, MN: Liturgical Press, 1998), 398; Walter Bauer, "ὁδός," in *A Greek-English Lexicon of the New Testament and Other Early Christian Literature* (Chicago: University of Chicago Press, 1979), 554.

2. Ilia Delio, *Clare of Assisi: A Heart Full of Love* (Cincinnati, OH: St. Anthony Messenger Press, 2007), Kindle edition, loc 1140–45.

3. Bauer, "μετανοέω," *Greek-English Lexicon*, 511–12. See also Strong's Concordance "metanoeó," https://biblehub.com/greek/3340.htm, accessed September 30, 2018.

4. Stanley Hauerwas, *Cross-Shattered Christ: Meditations on the Seven Last Words* (Grand Rapids, MI: Brazos Press, 2004), 59–66.

5. Ibid., 83–90.

6. Ibid., 95–102.

7. A 2013 study from the University of Southern California's Marshall School of Business estimated that people in the US would consume approximately 15.5 hours of media per person per day by the year 2015. Given a linear rate of growth calculated from the study's projections (which would be quite a conservative estimate given the ubiquity of media today!), that number would equate to approximately 17.5 hours per person per day at the time of this work! Julie Riggot, "Americans Consume Media in a Major Way, Study Finds," USC News, October 30, 2013, https://news.usc.edu/56894/americans-consume-media-in-a-major-way-study-finds/, accessed September 30, 2018.

8. Ilia Delio, *Making All Things New: Catholicity, Cosmology, Consciousness* (Maryknoll, NY: Orbis Books, 2015), 159.

9. Thomas Merton, *The Inner Experience: Notes on Contemplation* (New York: HarperOne, 2003), 21.

10. Bernadette Roberts, *The Christian Contemplative Journey: Essays on the Path* (Austin, TX: ContemplativeChristians.com, 2017), 204.

11. E. Kadloubovsky and G. E. H. Palmer, eds., *Writings from the Philokalia on Prayer of the Heart* (London: Faber and Faber, 1951, 1992), 140–41.

12. Ibid., 138.

13. Ibid., 110.

14. Lisa Lombardi, ed., *Mindfulness: The New Science of Health and Happiness* (New York: Time Inc. Books, 2017).

15. Mary Elizabeth Williams, "Why Every Mind Needs Mindfulness," in *Mindfulness: The New Science of Health and Happiness*, 13–14.

16. Hauerwas, *Cross-Shattered Christ*, 63. Cynthia Bourgeault also speaks to this action as a movement of *perichoresis*—an outpouring of love typical of the Trinitarian nature of God. Cynthia Bourgeault, *The Wisdom Jesus: Transforming Heart and Mind—A New Perspective on Christ and His Message* (Boston: Shambhala Publications, 2008), 71ff.

17. Bonnie Thurston and Judith Ryan, *Philippians and Philemon*, Sacra Pagina New Testament Commentary Series, vol. 10 (Collegeville, MN: Liturgical Press, 2005), 91.

18. Bourgeault, *The Wisdom Jesus*, 142. Cf. Bourgeault, *Centering Prayer and Inner Awakening* (Lanham, MD: Cowley Publications, 2004), 87–88.

19. Bernadette Roberts, *What Is Self? A Study of the Spiritual Journey in Terms of Consciousness* (Boulder, CO: Sentient Publications, 2005), 68. We should note that what remains is *not* what Parker Palmer terms an "empty self," one that consists of a void that allows for "competitive success, consumerism, sexism, racism, or anything that might give . . . the illusion of being better than others." Parker Palmer, *A Hidden Wholeness: The Journey toward an Undivided Life* (San Francisco: Jossey-Bass, 2004), 38.

20. Theologian Walter Brueggemann places the psalms in three major classes: *orientation*, *disorientation*, and *reorientation*. Laments such as Psalm 22 fall in the middle category. Walter Brueggemann, *Praying the Psalms: Engaging Scripture and the Life*

of the Spirit (Eugene, OR: Cascade Books, 2007), 8–11. Cf. Walter Brueggemann, *The Message of the Psalms: A Theological Commentary* (Minneapolis: Augsburg, 1984), 19–23; Patrick Woodhouse, *Life in the Psalms: Contemporary Meaning in Ancient Texts* (London: Bloomsbury Continuum, 2015), 253–54.

21. Athanasius, *On the Incarnation* (New Kensington, PA: Whitaker House, 2016).

22. Kathleen Stassen Berger, *The Developing Person: Through the Life Span* (New York: Worth Publishers, 2008), 182. Cf. Bernadette Roberts, *The Experience of No-Self: A Contemplative Journey* (Albany: State University of New York Press, 1993), 38.

23. Beatrice Bruteau, "Prayer and Identity," in *Spirituality, Contemplation and Transformation: Writings on Centering Prayer*, ed. Thomas Keating (Brooklyn, NY: Lantern Books, 2008), 89–95. Relatedly, author Parker Palmer notes that the age-old question of "Who am I?" cannot be understood apart from the answer to the inquiry of "Whose am I?" The tether between the two is the reality that "there is no selfhood outside of relationship." Parker Palmer, *Let Your Life Speak: Listening for the Voice of Vocation* (San Francisco: Jossey-Bass, 2000), 17.

24. Bruteau, "Prayer and Identity," 98–99.

25. Theologian N. T. Wright notes that through Christ's work we become "colleagues and partners" in the renewal of creation— "God's ultimate purpose." N. T. Wright, *Surprised by Hope: Rethinking Heaven, the Resurrection, and the Mission of the Church* (New York: HarperOne, 2008), 192.

26. Delio, *Making All Things New*, 83.

27. John of the Cross, *The Collected Works of St. John of the Cross*, trans. by Kieran Kavanaugh and Otilio Rodriguez (Washington, DC: ICS Publications, 1991), 353–57.

28. Ilia Delio, *The Unbearable Wholeness of Being: God, Evolution, and the Power of Love* (Maryknoll, NY: Orbis Books, 2013), Kindle edition, loc 1983. Bourgeault says of this "storm" that the "practice of meditational prayer loosens repressed material in the unconscious, the initial fruits of spiritual practice may not be the expected peace and enlightenment, but destabilization and the emergence into consciousness of considerable pain." Bourgeault, *Centering Prayer and Inner Awakening*, 97.

29. *Philokalia*, 140.

30. Merton expands on Paul's words, writing that we must radically excise "everything that is focused on our exterior and self-centered passion as self-assertion, greed, lust; as the desire for the survival and perpetuation of our illusory and superficial self, to the detriment of our interior and true self." Merton, *The Inner Experience*, 41.

31. Roberts, *What Is Self?* 62. Abhishiktananda adds due depth to Roberts' assertion: "God cannot be an *object*, because by definition an object depends on a *subject*, who sets it before himself...so as to be able to look at it or deal with it.... We cannot rightly speak of God in the third person, despite the exigencies of grammatical or linguistic convention. God comes *first*. I am only myself in the *thou* which God addresses to me. God alone is first person, in the proper sense of the term, for he is the fount of all discourse. Genuine experience of the Presence requires that God should be met as the first person, as *I*. Abhishiktananda, *Prayer* (London: Canterbury Press Norwich, 1967, 2006), 81.

32. Kieran Kavanaugh, introduction to "The Dark Night" in *John of the Cross*, 356.

33. Joseph Chilton Pearce, *The Biology of Transcendence: A Blueprint of the Human Spirit* (Rochester, VT: Park Street Press, 2002), 210.

34. *Philokalia*, 137.

35. Delio, *The Unbearable Wholeness of Being*, loc 1961–66.

36. Delio, *Clare of Assisi*, loc 1111.

37. Henri Nouwen, Donald McNeill, and Douglas Morrison, *Compassion: A Reflection on the Christian Life* (New York: Image Books, 1982), 27–28.

38. Ibid., 106–7. Cf. Laird, *Into the Silent Land*, 115–16.

39. *Oxford English Dictionary*, s.v. "as," https://en.oxforddictionaries.com/definition/as, accessed October 6, 2018.

40. Cf. Bourgeault, *The Heart of Centering Prayer*, 93; Pennington, *Centering Prayer*, 119ff.

41. Martin Laird, *Into the Silent Land: The Practice of Contemplation* (London: Darton, Longman, and Todd, 2006), 10.

42. Ellen Birx, *Selfless Love: Beyond the Boundaries of Self and Other* (Boston: Wisdom Publications, 2014), 130. Cf. Roberts, *The Experience of No-Self*, 29.

43. Cf. Bruteau, "Prayer and Identity," 110.

44. Merton, *The Inner Experience*, 22.

45. Cf. Delio, *Making All Things New*, 155. This kind of relational living also gives rise to the kind of relationality-responsibility ethics that ethicist Charles Curran advocates, where people are simultaneously in relationship with "God, neighbor, world, and self." Charles Curran, *The Catholic Moral Tradition Today: A Synthesis* (Washington, DC: Georgetown University Press, 1999), 73–77.

46. Bruteau, "Prayer and Identity," 111. Abhishiktananda is tuned into the same vision: "I never truly meet God when I think of him as object, but rather only in the depth of a purified experience of my own *I*, which is a participation in the unique divine I. To be absolutely true, the *Thou* of my prayer should be grounded in the *Thou* which the Son eternally addresses to the Father, in the indivisible I-Thou of the One-in-Three." Abhishiktananda, *Prayer*, 81.

47. Richard Rohr, *Eager to Love: The Alternative Way of Francis of Assisi* (Cincinnati, OH: Franciscan Media, 2014), 163. The themes here (as in Delio's work) resonate strongly with the ideas of the twentieth-century priest Pierre Teilhard de Chardin. As an example, see his discussions on the "Omega Point" in his work *Man's Place in Nature* (Toronto: R. P. Pryne, 2015), Kindle; cf. Delio, *The Unbearable Wholeness of Being*, loc 1575–620.

48. Cf. Daniel Migliore, *Faith Seeking Understanding: An Introduction to Christian Theology* (Grand Rapids, MI: William B. Eerdmans, 1991), 152–54.

49. Wright, *Surprised by Hope*, 199.

50. Roberts, *The Experience of No-Self*, 146–50.

51. Delio, *Making All Things New*, 162.

52. Wright, *Surprised by Hope*, 204.

Conclusion

1. Ilia Delio, *Making All Things New: Catholicity, Cosmology, Consciousness* (Maryknoll, NY: Orbis Books, 2015), 157.

2. John Main, *The Heart of Creation* (London: Canterbury Press Norwich, 2007), Kindle edition, loc 541–45.

3. Merton notes that a psychological awareness of self fits in the "natural," while awareness of God is impossible without

"supernatural" engagement. Thomas Merton, *The Inner Experience: Notes on Contemplation* (New York: HarperOne, 2003), 12.

4. *Symeon the New Theologian: The Discourses*, trans. C. J. de Catanzaro (Mahwah, NJ: Paulist Press, 1980), "Discourse 32," 336.

5. John Wesley, "The Means of Grace," in *John Wesley's Sermons: An Anthology*, ed. Albert Outler and Richard Heitzenrater (Nashville: Abingdon Press, 1991), 160.

6. Robert Benson, *Living Prayer* (New York: Jeremy P. Tarcher/Penguin, 1999), 88.

7. Henri Nouwen, *Spiritual Formation: Following the Movements of the Spirit* (New York: HarperOne, 2010), xx–xxi. For a broader discussion on the shortcomings of spiritual formation of both clergy and the churches, see L. Gregory Jones, "Beliefs, Desires, Practices, and the Ends of Theological Education," in *Practicing Theology: Beliefs and Practices in Christian Life*, ed. Miroslav Volf and Dorothy Bass (Grand Rapids, MI: William B. Eerdmans, 2002), 185–205. Cf. David Keller, "Binding Head and Heart: A Conversation Concerning Theological Education: The Contemplative Ministry Project," in *Spirituality, Contemplation and Transformation: Writings on Centering Prayer*, ed. Thomas Keating (Brooklyn, NY: Lantern Books, 2008), 167–71.

8. Benson, *Living Prayer*, 79.

9. Elaine A. Heath and Larry Duggins, *Missional. Monastic. Mainline: A Guide to Starting Micro-Communities in Historically Mainline Traditions* (Eugene, OR: Cascade Books, 2014), 41–42.

10. Alan J. Roxburgh and M. Scott Boren, *Introducing the Missional Church: What It Is, Why It Matters, and How to Become One* (Grand Rapids, MI: Baker, 2009), 45.

11. Keller, "Binding Head and Heart," 167.

Glossary

Active prayer: a discursive type of contemplative prayer in which the participant "actively" engages the mind to process revelatory content.

Apatheia: a state of calmed thoughts and desires that aid in humanity's truest purpose of pursuing God; a passionless condition that does not extract itself from the world, but instead allows for love to flow freely in compassion toward and in unity with God's creation.

Association areas: geographical centers in the temporal, parietal, and occipital lobes of the brain that aggregate and analyze information to help form perceptions.

Atonement: the reconciling work of Christ's life, death, and resurrection.

Brain: the aggregate of physical structures consisting of hundreds of millions of neurons that collect and process sensory, cognitive, and emotional data.

Centering Prayer: a contemplative prayer practice as constructed by Thomas Keating, William Meninger, and the late M. Basil Pennington. This apophatic discipline of putting aside physical, mental, and spiritual distractions is rooted in the theological idea of *kenosis*, imitating Jesus's "emptying out" of his divine estate and instead choosing humility, selflessness, and death.

Compassion: a state of solidarity in suffering with something or someone else. In Christ, we suffer alongside others via a state of *ex abundantia*, that is, out of an overabundance of love through which we can share ourselves.

Contemplatio ("contemplation"): the final of four stages of the classic view of *lectio divina* ("divine reading"); this phase represents a place unbound by the human concepts of time or space, characterized by a profound encounter grounded in God.

Contemplation: in a Christian context, a term that typically implies a non-discursive residing in the Divine Presence. In this work, it expands to include a mindful approach to all forms of prayer, an awareness of God as the loving force undergirding all existence.

Contemplative prayer: see contemplation.

Detachment: see *Apatheia*.

Dispassionate: see *Apatheia*.

Dualism: a worldview predicated on a subject/object perception of the world. This view creates a de facto partition or separation between ourselves—the subjects—and those persons or things we see as "outside" of us—the objects. By default, we as subjects tend to objectify anything perceived in this way, including God.

Examen: a contemplative prayer technique promoted by Ignatius of Loyola in which the pray-er reflects on experiences of the day past, and then envisions loving outcomes of the day to come. The *examen* is open to numerous modifications, but all are based on the idea of praying experiences and inviting God to serve as our "Divine Therapist."

Heart: in the traditional sense, that central part of us that grounds our thoughts, emotions, desires, and will. It is the part of us that most closely resembles the image and likeness of God.

Illumination: the second of three traditional phases of the contemplative life in which the contemplative consciously experiences God's revelatory grace and knowledge; this stage is typically preceded by *purgation* and is followed by the third step of *union*.

Image of God: while humanity is created in the image of God, Christ reflects the true glory of God, and as such is the true Image of the Divine. Humanity, then, is created in the image of the Image.

Imaginative prayer: a form of contemplative prayer taking its lead from Ignatius of Loyola's *Spiritual Exercises* that invites the pray-er to enter God's reality through scenes of scripture or other spiritual devices. The pray-er is encouraged to fully engage with all the senses—seeing, hearing, smelling, tasting, and touching.

Jesus Prayer: a contemplative "mantra" in which the pray-er repeats some form of "Lord Jesus Christ, Son of God, have mercy upon me, a sinner." This type of prayer was commonly present in the Orthodox traditions of the church.

Kenosis: the act of "emptying out," especially as exemplified through Jesus's selfless and humble act of parting with his divine estate and enduring his passion and death (Phil 2:5–11).

Lectio (**"reading"**): the first of four stages of the classic view of *lectio divina* ("divine reading") in which the pray-er receives divine revelation through reading, hearing, or some other means.

Lectio divina (**"divine reading"**): an ancient Christian practice of praying the scriptures, consisting of reading a passage (*lectio*), meditating on that text or a subsection (*meditatio*), praying through the experience of the meditation (*oratio*), and finally moving into the non-activity of simply being in God's Presence (*contemplatio*).

Meditatio ("**meditation**"): the second of four stages of *lectio divina* ("divine reading") whereby the one who prays intellectually digests the biblical passage that has been read, paying particular attention to some part that emerges as central to the pray-er's current context.

Mind: the faculty of awareness of experiences, thoughts, and feelings, as a result of the processes of the brain; how the brain "sees" itself.

"Mind of Christ": a mind that conforms to the disposition of Jesus, characterized by a sense of humility and selflessness. Ultimately "other"-oriented, those with this mind perceive a unitive state of limitless, loving intimacy and compassion.

Nature walk: when defined as contemplative prayer, a form of *visio divina* ("divine seeing") in which creation becomes the divine canvass onto which is painted the glory of God.

Neuroplasticity: the brain's ability to forge new connections and/or restructure itself given the right stimuli, leading to novel ways of thinking and experiential interpretations, which ultimately can influence the formation of different perceptions.

Oratio ("**prayer**"): the third of four stages of *lectio divina* ("divine reading") in which the contemplative begins to pray through the experience of his or her meditation on scripture through praise, lament, etc.

Passive prayer: in contrast to "active prayer," a non-discursive type of contemplative prayer in which the participant attempts an apophatic approach, focusing on God via "open" mindfulness.

Perception: an interpretation of the world that combines some sensual input (sight, sound, smell, etc.) along with memories, emotions, and context to form a final impression of "reality."

Perichoresis: the mutual indwelling of the persons of God within God's self, and the loving, "circular dance" thereof.

Praying Psalms: the act of adopting the psalms as a prayer book, claiming the tones of the praises, thanksgivings, or laments found therein as our own; entering into the psalmists' world.

Purgation: the process of the preparatory cleansing of the heart, including but not limited to the elimination of psychological and emotional distractions in an attempt to make room for the indwelling of God; the first of three traditional phases of the contemplative life that also includes *illumination* and *union*.

Purity of heart: while sometimes used synonymously with *apatheia*, this term, preserved by the Orthodox tradition, is better equated with the singular focus on God and the loving and compassionate attitudes that result from that divine attention.

Self-death/identity-resurrection theory: an atonement theory (of the author's creation) which asserts that, on the cross, Jesus literally underwent a process of dying to the ego "self" (*self-death*) that tends to falsely objectify and divide, and upon his resurrection, he emerged with a new self-identity (*identity-resurrection*) as one knowingly inseparable from the love of God the Father through the Spirit. This redeeming act paved the way for all humanity; and since we are grafted into this same body of Christ, we too must undergo the same process in our lives.

Spirit (human): the part of human reality that is capable of communicating with and experiencing the Ultimate Reality; our truest, core selves.

Spiritual Exercises: a compilation of contemplative disciplines including meditations, prayers, and practices created by the sixteenth-century mystic Ignatius Loyola; he designed them to deepen the practitioner's relationship with God.

Union: an experience of "oneness" with God, specifically as a result of divine contemplation. In the Christian tradition, this union is not a "return" to the source but instead an experience of love so enveloping as to render God and the pray-er indistinguishable from each other; this contemplative experience is classically preceded by the preparatory stages of *purgation* and *illumination*.

Unitive perception: the means of seeing holistically, resisting the natural tendency for our divisive brain to dominate, but deferring to that part of us that takes in the whole; seeing as God might see.

Bibliography

Abhishiktananda. *Prayer*. London: Canterbury Press Norwich, 2006. First published 1967.

Abraham, William. "Symeon the New Theologian." In *The Oxford Handbook of the Epistemology of Theology*, edited by William Abraham and Frederick Aquino, 383–92. Oxford: Oxford University Press, 2017.

Alfeyev, Hilarion. *St. Symeon the New Theologian and Orthodox Tradition*. Oxford Early Christian Studies. Oxford: Oxford University Press, 2000.

Anderson, Douglas. "Neuroscience." In *The Wiley-Blackwell Companion to Christian Mysticism*, edited by Julia Lamm, 650–69. Malden, MA: John Wiley and Sons, 2012.

Andrews-Hanna, Jessica. "The Brain's Default Network and Its Adaptive Role in Mentation." *Neuroscientist* 18, no. 3 (2012): 251–70.

Athanasius. *On the Incarnation*. New Kensington, PA: Whitaker House, 2016.

Augustine of Hippo. *The Confessions*. Translated by Maria Boulding. Hyde Park, NY: New City Press, 2016. First published 1997.

Aurelius, Marcus. *Meditations*. Translated by George Long. Mineola, NY: Dover Publications, 1997.

Bain, Brian. "The Divine Light and Ecstasy in Religious and Near-Death Experiences: A Retrospective Glance and a

View for the Future." *Journal of Near-Death Studies* 24, no. 4 (2006): 191–254.

Ballenger, Isam E. "Ephesians 4:1–16." *Interpretation: A Journal of Bible and Theology* 51, no. 3 (July 1997): 292–95.

Balthasar, Hans Urs von. *Prayer*. San Francisco: Ignatius Press, 1986.

Barth, Karl. *Evangelical Theology: An Introduction*. Grand Rapids, MI: William B. Eerdmans, 1963.

Bauer, Walter. *A Greek-English Lexicon of the New Testament and Other Early Christian Literature*. Chicago: University of Chicago Press, 1979.

Beauregard, Mario, and Denyse O'Leary. *The Spiritual Brain: A Neuroscientist's Case for the Existence of the Soul*. New York: HarperOne, 2007.

Beauregard, Mario, and Vincent Paquette. "Neural Correlates of a Mystical Experience in Carmelite Nuns." *Neuroscience Letters* 405 (2006): 186–90.

Begley, Sharon. *The Plastic Mind*. London: Constable and Robinson, 2009.

Benedict of Nursia. *The Rule of Saint Benedict*. Translated by Anthony Meisel and M. L. del Mastro. New York: Doubleday, 1975.

Benitez-Burraco, Antonio. "How the Language We Speak Affects the Way We Think." *Psychology Today*. February 2, 2017. https://www.psychologytoday.com/us/blog/the-biolinguistic-turn/201702/how-the-language-we-speak-affects-the-way-we-think.

Benson, Robert. *Living Prayer*. New York: Jeremy P. Tarcher/Penguin, 1999.

Berger, Kathleen Stassen. *The Developing Person: Through the Life Span*. New York: Worth Publishers, 2008.

Berkovich-Ohana, Aviva, Joseph Glicksohn, and Tal Dotan Ben-Soussan. "Creativity Is Enhanced by Long-Term Mindfulness Training and Is Negatively Correlated with Trait

Default-Mode-Related-Low-Gamma Inter-Hemispheric Connectivity." *Mindfulness* 8, no. 3 (2017): 717–27.

Birx, Ellen. *Selfless Love: Beyond the Boundaries of Self and Others.* Somerville, MA: Wisdom Publications, 2014.

Bloesch, Donald. *The Struggle of Prayer.* Colorado Springs: Helmers and Howard, 1988.

Boff, Leonardo. *The Lord's Prayer: The Prayer of Integral Liberation.* Maryknoll, NY: Orbis Books, 1983.

Bourgeault, Cynthia. "Beatrice Bruteau's 'Prayer and Identity': An Introduction with Text and Commentary." In *Spirituality, Contemplation and Transformation: Writings on Centering Prayer*, edited by Thomas Keating, 113–26. Brooklyn, NY: Lantern Books, 2008.

———. *Centering Prayer and Inner Awakening.* Lanham, MD: Cowley Publications, 2004.

———. *The Heart of Centering Prayer: Nondual Christianity in Theory and Practice.* Boulder, CO: Shambhala Publications, 2016.

———. *The Wisdom Jesus: Transforming Heart and Mind—A New Perspective on Christ and His Message.* Boston: Shambhala Publications, 2008.

Brewer, Judson, Patrick D. Worhunsky, Jeremy R. Gray, Yi-Yuan Tang, Jochen Weber, and Hedy Kober. "Meditation Experience Is Associated with Differences in Default Mode Network Activity and Connectivity." *Proceedings of the National Academy of Sciences of the United States of America* 108, no. 50 (2011): 20254–59.

Brueggemann, Walter. *Genesis.* Interpretation: A Bible Commentary for Teaching and Preaching. Atlanta, GA: John Knox Press, 1982.

———. *The Message of the Psalms: A Theological Commentary.* Minneapolis, MN: Augsburg, 1984.

———. *Praying the Psalms: Engaging Scripture and the Life of the Spirit.* Eugene, OR: Cascade Books, 2007.

Bruteau, Beatrice. "Prayer and Identity." In *Spirituality, Contemplation and Transformation: Writings on Centering Prayer*, edited by Thomas Keating, 84–112. Brooklyn, NY: Lantern Books, 2008.

Carson, Shelley. *Your Creative Brain*. San Francisco: Jossey-Bass, 2010.

Cassian, John. *The Works of John Cassian*. Translated by Edgar Gibson. Veritatis Splendor Publications, 2012.

Climacus, John. *The Ladder of Divine Ascent*. Toronto: Patristic Publishing, 2017.

Cloud, David. "Evangelicals Turning to Catholic 'Spirituality.'" July 30, 2008, last modified September 24, 2019. https://www.wayoflife.org/database/evangelicals_turning_to_catholic_spirituality.html.

The Cloud of Unknowing. Edited by Ira Progoff. New York: Delta Books, 1957.

Coe, John. "The Controversy over Contemplation and Contemplative Prayer: A Historical, Theological, and Biblical Resolution." *Journal of Spiritual Formation and Soul Care* 7, no. 1 (2014): 140–53.

Colzato, Lorenzo, Ayca Ozturk, and Bernhard Hommel. "Meditate to Create: The Impact of Focused-Attention and Open-Monitoring Training on Convergent and Divergent Thinking." *Frontiers in Psychology* 3, no. 116 (2012): 1–5.

Combs, Allan, and Stanley Krippner. "Process, Structure, and Form: An Evolutionary Transpersonal Psychology of Consciousness." *International Journal of Transpersonal Studies* 22, no. 1 (2003): 47–60.

———. "Spiritual Growth and the Evolution of Consciousness: Complexity, Evolution, and the Farther Reaches of Human Nature." *International Journal of Transpersonal Studies* 18, no. 1 (1999): 11–21.

———. "Structures of Consciousness and Creativity: Opening the Doors of Perception." In *Everyday Creativity and New Views of Human Nature: Psychological, Social, and Spiritual Perspectives*, edited by Ruth Richards, 131–49. Washington, DC: American Psychological Association, 2007.

Commission on World Mission and Evangelism, World Council of Churches. "Towards Common Witness to Christ Today: Mission and Visible Unity of the Church." *International Review of Mission* 99, no. 1 (April 2010).

Cousar, Charles. *The Letters of Paul.* Interpreting Biblical Texts. Nashville, TN: Abingdon Press, 1996.

Cousins, Ewert. "Preface to the Series." In *Christian Spirituality, Vol. 1: Origins to the Twelfth Century*, edited by Bernard McGinn, John Meyendorff, and Jean Leclercq, xi–xiv. New York: Crossroad, 1987.

Craddock, Fred B. *Philippians.* Interpretation: A Bible Commentary for Teaching and Preaching. Louisville, KY: Westminster John Knox Press, 1985.

Csikszentmihalyi, Mihaly. *Creativity: The Psychology of Discovery and Invention.* New York: Harper Perennial Modern Classics, 2013. First published 1996.

———. *Flow: The Psychology of Optimal Experience.* New York: Harper Perennial Modern Classics, 2008. First published 1990.

Curran, Charles. *The Catholic Moral Tradition Today: A Synthesis.* Washington, DC: Georgetown University Press, 1999.

Davies, Susan. "Relational Unity in Mission: Reflecting God's Life." *Journal of Ecumenical Studies* 45, no. 2 (2010): 234–44.

Delio, Ilia. *Clare of Assisi: A Heart Full of Love.* Cincinnati, OH: St. Anthony Messenger Press, 2007.

———. *Making All Things New: Catholicity, Cosmology, Consciousness.* Maryknoll, NY: Orbis Books, 2015.

————. *The Unbearable Wholeness of Being: God, Evolution, and the Power of Love*. Maryknoll, NY: Orbis Books, 2013.

Dionysius the Areopagite. *The Mystical Theology*. Translated by C. E. Rolt. Philadelphia: Dalcassian, 2017.

Eckhart, Meister. *True Hearing*. Translated by Claud Field. Grand Rapids, MI: Christian Classics Ethereal Library, n.d. http://www.ccel.org/ccel/eckhart/sermons.html (accessed November 24, 2017).

Edwards, Jonathan. *The Works of Jonathan Edwards, A. M.* Edited by Edward Hickman. London: Ball, Arnold, 1839.

Egan, Harvey. *An Anthology of Christian Mysticism*. Collegeville, MN: Liturgical Press, 1996.

Eliot, T. S. *Collected Poems, 1909–1962*. New York: Houghton Mifflin Harcourt, 1963.

Feldmeier, Peter. *Christian Spirituality: Lived Expressions in the Life of the Church*. Winona, MN: Anselm Academic, 2015.

Fox, Matthew. *Creativity: Where the Divine and the Human Meet*. New York: Tarcher/Putnam, 2002.

Gilbert, Paul. *The Compassionate Mind*. London: Robinson, 2013.

Goleman, Daniel. *Destructive Emotions: How Can We Overcome Them?* New York: Bantam Books, 2003.

Goleman, Daniel, and Richard Davidson. *Altered Traits: Science Reveals How Meditation Changes Your Mind, Brain, and Body*. New York: Avery, 2017.

Gregory of Nyssa. *The Life of Moses*. Translated by Abraham Malherbe and Everette Ferguson. New York: Paulist Press, 1978.

Hanson, Rick, and Richard Mendius. *Buddha's Brain: The Practical Neuroscience of Happiness, Love, and Wisdom*. Oakland: New Harbinger Publications, 2009.

Harmless, William. *Mystics*. New York: Oxford University Press, 2008.

Hartman, David, and Diane Zimberoff. "Higher Stages of Human Development." *Journal of Heart-Centered Therapies* 11, no. 2 (2008): 3–95.

Hauerwas, Stanley. *Cross-Shattered Christ: Meditations on the Seven Last Words*. Grand Rapids, MI: Brazos Press, 2004.

Hawthorne, Gerald F., Ralph Martin, and Daniel Reid, eds. *Dictionary of Paul and His Letters*. Downers Grove, IL: InterVarsity Press, 1993.

Hays, Richard B. *First Corinthians*. Interpretation: A Bible Commentary for Teaching and Preaching. Louisville, KY: Westminster John Knox Press, 2011.

Heath, Elaine, and Larry Duggins. *Missional. Monastic. Mainline: A Guide to Starting Micro-Communities in Historically Mainline Traditions*. Eugene, OR: Cascade Books, 2014.

Hobson, J. Allan. *The Chemistry of Conscious States: How the Brain Changes Its Mind*. Boston: Little, Brown, 1994.

Hooker, Morna. "Philippians." In *The New Interpreter's Bible*, 501. Nashville, TN: Abingdon Press, 2000.

Horan, Roy. "The Neuropsychological Connection between Creativity and Meditation." *Creativity Research Journal* 21, no. 2–3 (2009): 199–222.

Hunt, Hannah. *A Guide to St. Symeon the New Theologian*. Eugene, OR: Cascade Books, 2015.

Ignatius of Loyola. *The Spiritual Exercises*. Translated by Elder Mullan. New York: Magisterium Press, 2015.

Jang, Joon Hwan, Wi Hoon Jungb, Do-Hyung Kanga, and Min Soo Byuna. "Increased Default Mode Network Connectivity Associated with Meditation." *Neuroscience Letters*, no. 487 (2011): 358–62.

John of the Cross. *The Collected Works of St. John of the Cross*. Translated by Kieran Kavanaugh and Otilio Rodriguez. Washington, DC: ICS Publications, 1991.

John of Damascus. *Saint John of Damascus: Writings*. Translated by Frederic Chase. Ex Fontibus Company, 2015.

Jones, L. Gregory. "Beliefs, Desires, Practices, and the Ends of Theological Education." In *Practicing Theology: Beliefs and Practices in Christian Life*, edited by Miroslav Volf and

Dorothy Bass, 185–205. Grand Rapids, MI: William B. Eerdmans, 2002.

Joy, Melissa. "Time Travel through the Eternal Now." Wake Up World. Last modified February 20, 2015. https:// wakeup-world.com/2015/02/20/time-travel-through-the-eternal-now/.

Kadloubovsky, E., and G. E. H. Palmer, eds. *Writings from the Philokalia on Prayer of the Heart*. London: Faber and Faber, 1992. First published 1951.

Keller, David. "Binding Head and Heart: A Conversation Concerning Theological Education: The Contemplative Ministry Project." In *Spirituality, Contemplation and Transformation: Writings on Centering Prayer*, edited by Thomas Keating, 161–87. Brooklyn, NY: Lantern Books, 2008.

———. "Reading Living Water: The Integral Place of Contemplative Prayer in Christian Transformation." In *Spirituality, Contemplation and Transformation: Writings on Centering Prayer*, edited by Thomas Keating, 127–59. Brooklyn, NY: Lantern Books, 2008.

Kenney, John. *The Mysticism of Saint Augustine: Rereading the Confessions*. New York: Routledge, 2005.

Kinnard, Isabelle. "*Imitatio Christi* in Christian Martyrdom and Asceticism: A Critical Dialogue." In *Asceticism and Its Critics: Historical Accounts and Comparative Perspectives*, edited by Oliver Freiberger, 131–52. Oxford: Oxford University Press, 2006.

Laird, Martin. *Into the Silent Land: The Practice of Contemplation*. London: Darton, Longman, and Todd, 2006.

Lippelt, Dominique, Bernhard Hommel, and Lorenzo Colzato. "Focused Attention, Open Monitoring and Lovingkindness Meditation: Effects on Attention, Conflict Monitoring, and Creativity—A Review." *Frontiers in Psychology* 5, 1083 (September 2014): 1–5.

Lombardi, Lisa, ed. *Mindfulness: The New Science of Health and Happiness*. New York: Time Inc. Books, 2017.

Main, John. *The Heart of Creation*. London: Canterbury Press Norwich, 2007.

Maloney, George A. *The Mystic of Fire and Light: St. Symeon, the New Theologian*. Denville, NJ: Dimension Books, 1975.

———. *Pseudo-Macarius: The Fifty Spiritual Homilies and the Great Letter*. Mahwah, NJ: Paulist Press, 1992.

Maslow, Abraham. *The Farther Reaches of Human Nature*. New York: Penguin Books, 1993. First published 1971.

———. *Religions, Values, and Peak Experiences*. New York: Penguin Books, 1970, 1994.

McGinn, Bernard. *The Foundations of Mysticism: Origins to the Fifth Century*. New York: Crossroad, 1991.

McGuckin, John. "Symeon the New Theologian's Hymns of Divine Eros: A Neglected Masterpiece of the Christian Mystical Tradition." *Spiritus: A Journal of Christian Spirituality* 5, no. 2 (2005): 182–202.

McInnes, Jim. "Theodidact: Symeon the New Theologian's Claim to Be Taught by God." *Journal of Medieval Religious Cultures* 38, no. 2 (2012): 193–210.

Merton, Thomas. *Contemplative Prayer*. New York: Image Books, 1969, 1996.

———. *The Inner Experience: Notes on Contemplation*. New York: HarperOne, 2003.

Migliore, Daniel. *Faith Seeking Understanding: An Introduction to Christian Theology*. Grand Rapids, MI: William B. Eerdmans, 1991.

Moloney, Francis. *John*. Sacra Pagina New Testament Commentary Series, vol. 4. Collegeville, MN: Liturgical Press, 1998.

Newberg, Andrew. *Neurotheology: How Science Can Enlighten Us about Spirituality*. New York: Columbia University Press, 2018.

Newberg, Andrew, Eugene D'Aquili, and Vince Rause. *Why God Won't Go Away: Brain Science and the Biology of Belief*. New York: Ballantine Books, 2001.

Newberg, Andrew, Michael Pourdehnad, Abass Alavi, and Eugene D'Aquili. "Cerebral Blood Flow during Meditative Prayer: Preliminary Findings and Methodological Issues." *Perceptual Motor Skills* 97 (2003): 625–30.

Newberg, Andrew, and Mark Waldman. *How God Changes Your Brain: Breakthrough Findings from a Leading Neuroscientist*. New York: Ballantine Books, 2009.

Nouwen, Henri. *Discernment: Reading the Signs of Daily Life*. New York: HarperOne, 2013.

———. *Spiritual Formation: Following the Movements of the Spirit*. New York: HarperOne, 2010.

Nouwen, Henri, Donald McNeill, and Douglas Morrison. *Compassion: A Reflection on the Christian Life*. New York: Image Books, 1982.

O'Day, Gail. "John." In *The New Interpreter's Bible*, 493–865. Nashville, TN: Abingdon Press, 1995.

Origen. "De Principii." In *The Complete Works of Origen*. Translated by Philip Schaff. Toronto, 2016.

Osiek, Carolyn. "Philippians." In *The Catholic Study Bible*, 475–78. Oxford: Oxford University Press, 2006.

Paintner, Christine, and Lucy Wynkop. *Lectio Divina: Contemplative Awakening and Awareness*. New York: Paulist Press, 2008.

Palamas, Gregory. *The Triads*. Translated by John Meyendorff. New York: Paulist Press, 1983.

Palmer, Parker J. *A Hidden Wholeness: The Journey toward an Undivided Life*. San Francisco, CA: Jossey-Bass, 2004.

———. *Let Your Life Speak: Listening for the Voice of Vocation*. San Francisco, CA: Jossey-Bass, 2000.

Pearce, Joseph Chilton. *The Biology of Transcendence: A Blueprint of the Human Spirit*. Rochester, VT: Park Street Press, 2002.

Pennington, M. Basil. *Centering Prayer: Renewing an Ancient Christian Prayer Form*. New York: Image Books, 2001.

Ponticus, Evagrius. *The Praktikos. Chapters on Prayer.* Translated by John Bamberger. Cistercian Studies, vol. 4. Trappist, KY: Cistercian Publications, 1972.

Randall, John. "The Theme of Unity in John 17:20–23." *Ephemerides Theologicae Lovanienses* 41 (January 1965): 373–94.

Richards, Ruth. "Twelve Potential Benefits of Living More Creatively." In *Everyday Creativity and New Views of Human Nature: Psychological, Social, and Spiritual Perspectives*, edited by Ruth Richards, 289–319. Washington, DC: American Psychological Association, 2007.

Riggot, Julie. "Americans Consume Media in a Major Way, Study Finds." USC News. October 30, 2013. https://news.usc.edu/56894/americans-consume-media-in-a-major-way-study-finds/.

Roberts, Bernadette. *The Christian Contemplative Journey: Essays on the Path.* Austin, TX: ContemplativeChristians.com, 2017.

———. *The Experience of No-Self: A Contemplative Journey.* Albany: State University of New York Press, 1993.

———. *What Is Self? A Study of the Spiritual Journey in Terms of Consciousness.* Boulder, CO: Sentient Publications, 2005.

Robertson, David, Italo Biaggioni, Geoffrey Burnstock, Phillip Low, and Julian Paton, eds. *Primer on the Autonomic Nervous System.* Waltham, MA: Academic Press, 2012.

Rohr, Richard. *Eager to Love: The Alternative Way of Francis of Assisi.* Cincinnati, OH: Franciscan Media, 2014.

Rosen, Richard. *Original Yoga: Rediscovering Traditional Practices of Hatha Yoga.* Boston: Shambhala Publications, 2012.

Roxburgh, Alan, and M. Scott Boren. *Introducing the Missional Church: What It Is, Why It Matters, and How to Become One.* Grand Rapids, MI: Baker, 2009.

Schwartz, Jeffrey, and Sharon Begley. *The Mind and the Brain: Neuroplasticity and the Power of Mental Force.* New York: ReganBooks, 2002.

Senior, D. P., and Daniel Harrington. *1 Peter, Jude and 2 Peter.* Sacra Pagina New Testament Commentary Series, vol. 15. Collegeville, MN: Liturgical Press, 2003.

"Silent and Solo: How Americans Pray." August 15, 2017. https://www.barna.com/research/silent-solo-americans-pray/ (accessed September 1, 2018).

Sloyan, Gerard. *John.* Interpretation: A Bible Commentary for Teaching and Preaching. Louisville, KY: Westminster John Knox Press, 2009.

Sommerfeldt, John. *Bernard of Clairvaux on the Life of the Mind.* Mahwah, NJ: Paulist Press, 2004.

Stethatos, Niketas. *The Life of Saint Symeon the New Theologian.* Translated by Richard Greenfield. Cambridge, MA: Harvard University Press, 2013.

Sweeney, Michael S. *Brain: The Complete Mind.* Washington, DC: National Geographic Society, 2009.

Symeon the New Theologian. *Hymns of Divine Love.* Translated by George A. Maloney. Denville, NJ: Dimension Books, 1976.

Symeon the New Theologian: The Discourses. Translated by C. J. de Catanzaro. Mahwah, NJ: Paulist Press, 1980.

Taylor, Veronique, Veronique Daneault, Joshua Grant, et al. "Impact of Meditation Training on the Default Mode Network during a Restful State." *Social Cognitive and Affective Neuroscience* 8, no. 1 (2013): 4–14.

Teilhard de Chardin, Pierre. *Man's Place in Nature.* Toronto: R. P. Pryne, 2015.

Teresa, Mother. *In the Heart of the World: Thoughts, Stories and Prayers.* Novato, CA: New World Library, 1997.

Thibodeaux, Mark. *Reimagining the Ignatian Examen: Fresh Ways to Pray from Your Day.* Chicago: Loyola Press, 2015.

Thurston, Bonnie, and Judith Ryan. *Philippians and Philemon.* Sacra Pagina New Testament Commentary Series, vol. 10. Collegeville, MN: Liturgical Press, 2005.

Tomaino, Charlotte. *Awakening the Brain: The Neuropsychology of Grace.* New York: Atria Books, 2012.

Tortora, Gerard J., and Bryan H. Derrickson. *Principles of Anatomy and Physiology.* Hoboken, NJ: John Wiley and Sons, 2014.

Tradigo, Alfredo. *Icons and Saints of the Eastern Orthodox Church.* Los Angeles: J. Paul Getty Museum, 2006.

Twombly, Charles. *Perichoresis and Personhood: God, Christ, and Salvation in John of Damascus.* Eugene, OR: Pickwick Publications, 2015.

Underhill, Evelyn. *Mysticism.* New York: Image Books, 1990.

Vartanian, Oshin. "Attention, Cognitive Flexibility, and Creativity: Insights from the Brain." In *Creativity and Reason in Cognitive Development,* edited by James Kaufman and John Baer, 246–58. New York: Cambridge University Press, 2016.

Vartanian, Oshin, and Vinod Goel. "Neural Correlates of Creative Cognition." In *Evolutionary and Neurocognitive Approaches to Aesthetics, Creativity and the Arts,* edited by Colin Martindale et al., 195–207. Amityville, NY: Baywood Publishing, 2007.

Viskontas, Indre, and Bruce Miller. "Art and Dementia: How Degeneration of Some Brain Regions Can Lead to New Creative Impulses." In *Neuroscience of Creativity,* edited by Oshin Vartanian, Adam S. Bristol, and James C. Kaufman, 115–32. Cambridge, MA: MIT Press, 2013.

Wachholtz, Amy B., and Kenneth I. Pargament. "Is Spirituality a Critical Ingredient of Meditation? Comparing the Effects of Spiritual Meditation, Secular Meditation, and Relaxation on Spiritual, Psychological, Cardiac, and Pain Outcomes." *Journal of Behavioral Medicine* 28, no. 4 (August 2005): 369–84. https://doi: 10.1007/s10865-005-9008-5.

Wallace, B. Alan. *Contemplative Science: Where Buddhism and Neuroscience Converge.* New York: Columbia University Press, 2007.

———. *Hidden Dimensions: The Unifications of Physics and Consciousness*. New York: Columbia University Press, 2007.

Ware, Kallistos. *The Jesus Prayer*. London: Incorporated Catholic Truth Society, 2014.

Ware, Timothy. *The Orthodox Church*. London: Penguin Books, 1997. First published 1963.

Wesley, John. *John Wesley's Sermons: An Anthology*. Edited by Albert Outler and Richard Heitzenrater. Nashville, TN: Abingdon Press, 1991.

Westermann, Claus. *Praise and Lament in the Psalms*. Atlanta, GA: John Knox Press, 1981. First published 1965.

Wilbur, Ken. *Integral Spirituality*. Boston, MA: Integral Books, 2006.

Williams, Mary Elizabeth. "Why Every Mind Needs Mindfulness." In *Mindfulness: The New Science of Health and Happiness*, 8–15. New York: Time Inc. Books, 2017.

Woodhouse, Patrick. *Life in the Psalms: Contemporary Meaning in Ancient Texts*. London: Bloomsbury Continuum, 2015.

Wright, N. T. *Surprised by Hope: Rethinking Heaven, the Resurrection, and the Mission of the Church*. New York: HarperOne, 2008.

Yungen, Ray. *A Time of Departing: How Ancient Mystical Practices Are Uniting Christians with the World's Religions*. Eureka, MT: Lighthouse Trails Publishing, 2010.

Index